Moving Targets

Also by Stephen Kessler

Moving Targets
On Poets, Poetry & Translation

STEPHEN KESSLER

El León Literary Arts
Berkeley, California

Most of these essays, some in slightly different form, originally appeared in the following periodicals: *Bachy, The Bloomsbury Review, Calque, East Bay Express, Exquisite Corpse, Good Times, KUSP Review, North Bay Bohemian, Outlook, Poetry Flash, The Redwood Coast Review, San Francisco Review of Books, Santa Cruz Express,* and *The Sun* (Santa Cruz).

The author and publisher gratefully acknowledge the following for permission to reprint work quoted in this book: Harcourt, Inc. for lines from *Open Closed Open* by Yehuda Amichai, copyright 2000 by Yehuda Amichai, English translation copyright 2000 by Chana Bloch and Chana Kronfeld. HarperCollins Publishers for excerpts from *The Last Night of the Earth Poems* by Charles Bukowski, copyright 1992 by Charles Bukowski. HarperCollins Publishers for excerpts from *Hollywood* by Charles Bukowski, copyright 1989 by Charles Bukowski. HarperCollins Publishers for excerpts from *The Roominghouse Madrigals: Early Selected Poems 1946-1966* by Charles Bukowski, copyright 1960, 1962, 1963, 1965, 1968, 1988 by Charles Bukowski. HarperCollins Publishers for excerpts from *Septuagenarian Stew: Stories & Poems* by Charles Bukowski, copyright 1990 by Charles Bukowski. University of Pittsburgh Press for lines from "Lines Lost Among Trees" from *Picnic, Lightning* by Billy Collins, copyright 1988 by Billy Collins. New Directions Publishing Corp. for excerpts from *7 Greeks* by Guy Davenport, copyright 1995 by Guy Davenport. New Directions Publishing Corp. for excerpts from *Poems New and Selected* by James Laughlin, copyright 1938, 1945, 1959, 1969, 1970, 1978, 1982, 1983, 1984, 1985, 1986, 1987, 1988, 1989, 1990, 1992, 1994, 1995, 1996 by James Laughlin. New Directions Publishing Corp. for "The Mockingbird of Mockingbirds" from *Breathing the Water* by Denise Levertov, copyright 1987 by Denise Levertov.

El León Literary Arts is a private foundation established to extend the array of voices essential to a democracy's arts and education.

El León Literary Arts is distributed by Small Press Distribution, Inc., 800-869-7553; www.spdbooks.org.
El León books are also available on Amazon.com
El León web site: www.elleonliteraryarts.org

Publisher: Thomas Farber
Managing Editor: Kit Duane
Cover design: Andrea Young
Text design: Sara Glaser

ISBN 978-0-9795285-1-4

Library of Congress Control Number: 2008925998

for Daniela

Contents

Points Beyond

Back Home

Preface

These writings, spanning more than twenty-five years, together amount to a map of my enthusiasms and a personal journey through late-20th-century poetry. Beginning in California, my native region, and extending to the greater United States and points beyond, the essays examine the lives and works of a range of individuals whose contributions have been significant not just to me as a reader and writer but to the literary (and in some cases political) culture of our time.

The deep subjectivity of the best criticism is informed by the writer's reading, experience and sensibility. Where poetry is concerned, a sharp eye, a finely tuned ear and a certain analytical intuition are essential to any useful critical response. In my practice of literary journalism, or journalistic criticism, I've always tried to speak as plainly as possible to an intelligent nonspecialist reader interested in looking more deeply into the topic at hand. These essays were written not as an occasion for esoteric argument or as an exercise in theoretical discourse but in search of a more vital understanding that may expand the meaning of the merely "poetic."

Portraiture, memoir, cultural history, personal tribute, close reading—often a combination of these genres—the pieces collected here attempt to catch moments in the creative evolution of certain writers, to survey the trajectory and substance of their work, or to assess the achievement of a life recently ended. Reviews of books, reports on public appearances, examinations of style and ideas, of personas and personalities, also enter into the larger picture presented.

Despite the diversity of modes and poets, and variations in my thinking and perspective over the years, I find a surprising coherence and continuity in these pages—a consistent effort to see the subjects in their social, historical and biographical contexts, and to discern and reveal the essence of their accomplishment. The whole, I hope, in its exploration of the poet's role, and of the poets' individual voices and visions, amounts to an interpretive ecology, a poetics of eclectic appreciation, a vision of my own that may be of use to others.

—SK

Moving Targets

*Do you call those genteel little creatures American poets?
Do you term that perpetual, pistareen, paste-pot work,
American art, American drama, taste, verse? I think I hear,
echoed as from some mountaintop afar in the west, the
scornful laugh of the Genius of these States.*

WALT WHITMAN, *Democratic Vistas*

On Native Grounds

Rexroth Revisited

1 Pathfinder

In the fertile free-for-all of American letters there have been many excellent poets, but few have managed to alter the course of cultural history. Changes in sensibility tend to occur slowly, and no individual alone can be given credit for making these changes happen—yet certain artists appear from time to time whose work and presence catalyze others, opening the way for major breakthroughs. Kenneth Rexroth, who died last week at the age of seventy-six, was such an artist.

Rexroth's legendary San Francisco salon was the hothouse, proving ground and battlefield of at least two major literary movements of the 1940s and '50s. During that period his voice was also among the first to grace the noncommercial airwaves of radio station KPFA in Berkeley, a venture which he helped launch, where *Rexroth on Books*—improvised reviews recorded in the poet's home—appeared for many years. He helped resurrect for US audiences the ancient concept of poetry-as-performance and pioneered the hybrid form of poetry-and-jazz.

His concise and informative column "Classics Revisited"

was featured for a time in the *Saturday Review*—Rexroth was one of those nonacademic educators whose freewheeling zeal for sparking awareness gave conservative critics the shakes—and he was probably the only openly avowed anarchist ever to write political/cultural essays for a Hearst newspaper, as he did in his column for the *San Francisco Examiner* (a curious affiliation which provoked dismay among his lefty comrades). Rexroth's opinions were beyond left and right: he was a radically independent thinker.

His poetry is also hard to pin down. His published work dates from his early teens in Chicago, and though he experimented with current avant-garde techniques while coming of age, he evolved a very personal, speakable and accessible style that runs through all his writing up to the deep and simple clarities of his last poems, which bear the mark of his travels and studies in Japan. There is a strong religious and philosophical dimension, a meditative attention to the mysteries of existence, grounded in the sensuous universe of the body and its complex physical consciousness. Rexroth's poems are both abstract and erotic, pastoral and cosmopolitan, containing a phenomenal range of knowledge combined with a disarming directness of expression.

More than any other writer I can think of, he campaigned on a popular level for literature as a basis for world community, introducing countless international voices to North Americans, thereby breaking common human ground. His translation of Chinese and Japanese poets helped clear channels between East and West through which stimulating currents are still flowing.

However impressive all this may be (the catalog of his contributions goes on and on), it was more as a person than as a "figure" that Rexroth touched those who knew him. As a visitor to a couple of his Monday night soirees in Santa Barbara during the 1970s I was able to witness the poet in motion—pouring wine for his guests, telling jokes, gossiping, provoking people to read their latest efforts or discuss whatever—and was struck by his genuine interest in and respect for the individuals present. He could be cranky and opinionated, expounding for hours on virtually any subject, but there was also a playful lightness in his style of conversation that gave his salon an ebullient atmosphere. The sense of being dwarfed by his erudition, his studio's sagging bookcases crammed with thousands of tomes from every imaginable field of study, was offset by his contagious enthusiasm. Books or no books, he had a gift for opening the world.

It was this generosity toward other, usually younger poets—an ability to detect and nurture potential talent—that set him apart from other famous authors who wall themselves off behind a mystique of genius. For Rexroth, literature was a social art; it led to engagement with other people and encouragement of their native gifts. Countless writers from several generations are indebted to him for giving them a hand in finding their own way into their work and beyond.

Which isn't to say he was easy to get along with. His life was punctuated by personal and professional and political clashes with various friends and rivals. He was a master of the vituperative attack. Like many a high-powered artist, he had an ample ego and wasn't afraid to blow his own horn. But he also had the wisdom of humility, which runs continually through his poems along with the understanding that in the oneness of awakened vision the "self" is an illusion that disappears.

Painter, poet, self-taught scholar, astronomer, mountain climber, gadfly, cook, Rexroth was a walking embodiment of Emersonian versatility. His courage in following his own path led him through a creative realization that's nothing short of heroic. His life was an adventure in the making, an adventure now being carried on in the lives of those he inspired.

1982

2 *Salonkeeper*

In the 1970s, comfortably settled in Montecito, and no longer teaching his course on poetry and folk song at UC Santa Barbara, Kenneth Rexroth hosted a weekly salon on Monday evenings where a small group of young local poets—mostly women in their twenties—gathered to read poems, discuss writing and literature, drink wine, gossip and listen to Kenneth (as everyone called him) riff on all things considerable. Rexroth's mentorly flirtations and intellectual intercourse with his harem of disciples were graciously tolerated by his wife, the poet Carol Tinker, who after all had once been one herself. While Carol chain-smoked cigarettes and the master improvised on whatever subject came up for discussion, the guests felt engaged in something both intimate and historic, carrying on a rich tradition of Rexrothian social life.

It may have been a far cry from the seminal get-togethers of the 1940s and '50s where the San Francisco Renaissance and Beat movements were born, with Rexroth playing a similar role as ringleader and gadfly to an unruly and prodigiously gifted assortment of emerging writers, but the spirit of discourse and comradeship must have been comparable. Here was a cluster of bohemian types with artistic aspirations seeking mutual support and stimulation under the benevolent if somewhat irascible guidance of a giant who had long since proved his importance. As a poet, translator, critic, journalist and all-around cultural and political agitator, Rexroth was a monster of legendary proportions.

In the spring of 1976, on the first leg of a circuitous journey from Santa Cruz to Spain, my companion Hollis deLancey and I had the good timing to pass through Santa Barbara on the right day of the week and be invited by our local hosts to join them at the Rexroths' that evening. We were warned that the old man had not been in the best of health and had been rather grumpy lately, but the chance to meet him easily overrode any concern that he might be less than charming.

As it turned out, our presence seemed to perk him up. I was just getting started as a translator and Hollis, a painter, was studying Chinese, so those two connections with Kenneth's expertise appeared to lubricate his volubility. Just by being there, and being fairly talkative ourselves, we pumped fresh blood into the conversation, and Kenneth, energized by the transfusion, proceeded to edify and entertain us all with commentary on everything from García Lorca as a cabaret singer to the hand-shaking etiquette of East Asian diplomats. He seemed to take special pleasure in sharing gossip about Allen Ginsberg's early crisis of sexual identity—he'd come to Kenneth for counseling—and about Charles Mingus's self-proclaimed sexual exploits in his autobiography, *Beneath the Underdog*, explaining with full Rexrothian authority that Mingus was much too fat to have had more than a minuscule penis. He also remarked in passing on his disgust with Jack Kerouac's drunken boorishness and Charles Bukowski's despicable vulgarity.

We left his home that night delighted by our host's conviviality, inspired by his enthusiasms, and dazzled by the vast range of his knowledge and his effortless ability to move from the sublime to the scatological and back with equal engagement and authority. Rexroth was one of those rare know-it-alls who really did know it all and wasn't shy about letting you know he knew it. Anyone who has read his essays or heard tapes of his KPFA book review show, *Rexroth on Books*, where the critic would extemporaneously expound on whatever he'd been reading—you could hear him shuffling books in the background—can testify to his anti-academic erudition, his polymathic mastery and his freewheeling, freethinking willingness to risk the disapproval of friends and adversaries alike with his candid and informed opinions. Such intellectual courage was remarkable in the fifties and perhaps even rarer now.

But what I felt most personally that first evening and over the next few years of our occasional contact (he died in 1982) was his professional generosity, his sincere encouragement of anyone showing genuine interest in the creative path. Without explicitly commenting on or critiquing the poems of his acolytes, just by his attention and respect he egged them on. When I was an unknown translator trying to get a commission from Farrar, Straus and Giroux to do a version of one of Pablo Neruda's books, Kenneth wrote a personal letter recommending me to an editor there (alas, to no avail); it was a gesture graciously made, not because we were friends but because he thought I could do the job and was willing to put his own prestige on the line by endorsing my skills.

Beyond his accomplishments on paper, enough in themselves to leave a lasting mark as an artist, Rexroth remains a beacon, a model of the well-rounded literary life, a self-taught, straight-shooting nonspecialist who nevertheless mastered many disciplines ("Poets should never write prose except for money," he advised, yet his own prose is consistently interesting and provocative) and encouraged others to get on with the work. Those of us lucky enough to have had even minimal contact with him still carry in our consciousness the sparks he struck.

2003

Robert Duncan:
Living to Serve the Muse

White, wing-like sideburns flying from his temples, Robert Duncan stood at the podium in Stevenson Dining Hall, UC Santa Cruz, wearing a gorgeous gray wool cape and reading or singing his poems, marking the measure with his hand, rocking on the balls of his feet, moving his body as his voice moved saying the song, the audience moving along with him, going with the sound. It was December 1970, a difficult year for me. I'd spent the first six months in a half dozen madhouses up and down California, and the last six as depressed as I'd ever been, writing nothing—which is agony for an aspiring poet—and contemplating killing myself as I suffered through one last quarter of graduate school before bailing out for good. But Duncan was teaching a graduate seminar called Ideas of the Nature of Poetry, and knowing he was an important force I took the course.

At the end of the quarter he gave the reading in Stevenson, and for the first time I began to understand the musical base of his verse, which up to then had seemed so complex and incomprehensible to me, and his poems just opened up in their profusion of imagination, their spiritual lyricism, the range of consciousness from which they drew. Duncan took his vocation seriously—too seriously, one of his contemporaries told me—and put himself at the service of his muses, making his life a channel for poetry, for the unknown which rises to speak magic and transformation, and to confirm the presence of myth in the simplest events. His scholarship ranged across dozens of disciplines, whose associations he shared with about a dozen of us in his seminar, which mainly consisted of him coming in and talking about whatever was on his mind that morning, freely wandering from one subject to another but keeping the thread of the theme, poetry, and how it permeates the atmosphere of anyone who'll listen.

Through the gloom of my private depression I discerned flashes of clear light in Duncan's rap: he was spilling the beans on mysteries I was just coming back from—a scary adventure lost in the unconscious—unable to say where I'd been or was, feeling mute and stupid. His profoundly simple insights into the makings of poetry ("Trust your own voice") gave me a little courage to carry on, penetrated even my dull skull as we sat around and listened to him rave. Most of the other students took notes but mostly I just bathed in the waves of his giddy discourse, gossiping one minute about Gertrude Stein—with whom he shared roots in Oakland—and reflecting the next on meat orgies the cave people allegedly enjoyed before painting their walls, plunging into deliberate states of intoxication so as to free the beast that creates.

Robert was a great teacher because he communicated enthusiasm, he felt deeply what he was talking about and conveyed that feeling so clearly even a sad young man like me could be lifted by it. His words were a gift, his commitment an inspiration, so when he died at sixty-nine last week in San Francisco, even though I hadn't seen him in years and knew he was sick, it was saddening.

In a city of poets, Duncan was seen by many as the master. His mind was so alive, his learning so vast, his energy so intense—he was an intellectual monster who could write as powerfully about the flight of a butterfly as about the corruption of Lyndon Johnson at the height of the Vietnam War, could expound interpretations of Jungian psychology as readily as discuss contemporary television. He saw the form of the poem as an unfolding improvisation composed with the crisp decisiveness of a Zen brushstroke, only he used an electric typewriter, entering a field of action on the page where each keystroke counts in a continuous process, no going back. Once, in the Whole Earth restaurant at UCSC, reading to a few students, he came to a line that caused him to break down sobbing, his emotions were that close to the surface. His spontaneity made him real in a way more guarded artists rarely are.

When he was around twenty Robert worked for a while as personal secretary to Anaïs Nin. It was no doubt partly from her that he learned or had confirmed his sense of the individual life as an agent of legend, and that by writing one's re-imagined autobiography faithfully enough one could touch universal truths. At one point after he'd gained fame for his third major volume of verse, *Bending the Bow*, he vowed not to publish a book for fifteen years, so from the late 1960s to the early 1980s he kept a low literary profile except for an occasional reading. Poets aren't factories, I heard him say once; we're not obliged to produce at regular intervals a certain quantity of work. The process is more organic, or biological, or baroquely esoteric, linked to rhythms in the underworld, or in the astrological brilliance of the stars.

Synchronicity, the timely collision of lives, crossing of paths, intersections of experience, is a major motif in his work, his cross-eyed gaze taking in two planes at once as he associates naturally "rimes," or correspondences, among seemingly discrete happenings. He quoted Pound—"All ages are contemporaneous"—and proved it by living in ancient texts and bringing them up to date in his own days. Ahead of his time in many ways, he wrote proudly and passionately of his homosexuality long before such revelations were considered gay. The life of the poet was a heroic adventure, beyond hypocrisy, sublime.

Duncan's mother had died in childbirth and his father gave the baby up for adoption. That was in 1919. Sixty-two years later, in April 1981, Robert came to Santa Cruz for a reading, and by way of introduction to local poetry fans who might not be familiar with his work—or had been intimidated, as I had, by its expansive dimensions—I wrote a little piece in the *Santa Cruz Express* giving some background on the man and what he meant to me. In it I mentioned his date and place of birth, and that he was adopted. Shortly after the story came out I received a call from a woman who claimed to be his sister, whom he'd never met. She came to the reading that night and they were reunited.

There was a get-together afterward at the home of Nate Mackey and Gloria Watkins (also known as bell hooks), and Robert's sister, a few years older than he, proceeded to tell the assembled friends how she'd witnessed her brother's birth—seeing her mother die at the same time—and had been separated from her sibling ever since. So it was a strange and slightly eerie occasion, this gathering, fittingly mythic, both of them telling stories about their respective childhoods and subsequent development, acknowledging psychic parallels and common obscure or occult interests, Robert remarking with a mixture of glee and dismay that she was as nutty as he and therefore had to be for real. I was as stunned as anyone at my accidental role in this family drama, my election as Destiny's agent. It was his sister, Anne, who called me the other day to say he'd died.

I am no scholar of Robert's poetry. I've read only three or four of his books. But from those I've enhanced my understanding of language as a lyric dance, and of the imagination as a sacred zone where reality expands to its mythic dimensions. Duncan's work is romantic in the largest sense, embracing a breadth of praise and awe like Whitman's, extravagant and generous, testing the edges of excessiveness. He is undoubtedly among the major innovators of the age, a poet's poet whose spirit will shine happily in the lives of those who dare dive into his music, and make their own.

1988

Ferlinghetti: Canonized, but Not Co-opted

It was inevitable. Just as Bob Dylan has been turned into a marketing opportunity, and Jack Kerouac into a vehicle for beatnik kitsch, and the communist Frida Kahlo into an industry of tchotchkes, Lawrence Ferlinghetti the iconoclast has lasted long enough to have become canonical. The Pete Seeger of poetry, Ferlinghetti continues to fight valiantly for his own brand of anarcho-imaginative utopia in an America where even the cultural revolutionaries are routinely appropriated to promote capitalism.

Ferlinghetti is after all, and first of all, a successful businessman who has used his considerable skills in the marketplace to support his poetic and political passions. City Lights Books, both the landmark San Francisco store and the radical-vanguard publishing imprint, has managed to endure despite the corporate consolidation of literature and bookselling, a beacon of uppity independence. Banners hang on the side of its North Beach building calling for the president's impeachment, denouncing the war (and war in general) and invoking the voice of Pablo Neruda, another inspirational emblem of resistance and poet of the people. Ferlinghetti knows how to play with the big boys and, like Neruda, is a master propagandist but always with the charm and imagination and goofy dignity of the carnival barker: Step right up, folks, and get a load of this way-out poetry.

That Ferlinghetti has become an icon is ironic not least for the reverence increasingly accorded a poet whose own irreverence has been one of his signature qualities. The wry lightness of his style, its open opposition to the status quo, its impatience with hypocrisy and with the stupidities and brutalities of the powerful, its satiric wit and romantic vision of a more humane social order have been sustained over more than five decades of labor on the front lines of the culture wars. Now in his high eighties, he has proved that if you live long enough and keep on doing what you do well enough, even the most incorrigible rebel can become respectable. His survival itself is an accomplishment worthy of admiration, and when it's tied so closely to a continuing career as a poet, painter, publisher, bookseller and political agitator, the sustained energy of such an epic performance is awe-inspiring. Internationally adored as one of the few remaining stalwarts of a true counterculture, traveling frequently to book fairs and poetry festivals around the globe, garlanded with enough awards to burden even the staunchest spirit, Ferlinghetti presses on relentlessly with his campaign of questioning and protest and creation and celebration.

To San Francisco residents or frequenters of North Beach, the great man is a familiar sight, strolling down Columbus Avenue or sitting in the back of some neighborhood café reading a newspaper or even (as I witnessed summer before last) riding his bicycle along the Embarcadero on the way to a ballgame at SBC Park. The intimacy of the city is somehow embodied in the everyday presence of this practically mythic figure as just another local character. Not that he is particularly approachable: what may at first seem like a cool aloofness is, I've learned over the years, really just the reserve of a shy person. In my encounters with him, as someone in Bay Area poetry circles and a sometime City Lights author (they've published translations of mine), I've always found him low-key, abstractly friendly, courteous, sometimes engaged and forthcoming and sometimes detached or distracted, his mind on other things. But when working as the editor of his Pocket Poets Series, he is a no-nonsense hands-on professional, a tough negotiator of details, precise in his insights and forceful in his opinions.

His political opinions where poetry is concerned have sometimes struck me as simplistic, as when he claims that poets who don't actively in their writing oppose the crimes of the current administration are somehow complicit in them. This notion seems to me dangerously akin to the dubious idea that one is either "with us" or "with the terrorists." Such moral certainty is not typically characteristic of the greatest antiwar poets, from Wilfred Owen to Mahmoud Darwish, to name just two outstanding examples of witnesses who don't exempt themselves from what they're describing. Two of the twentieth century's most eloquent chroniclers of atrocity, Paul Celan and Czeslaw Milosz, assume a certain shame in humanity's crimes, and their poetry gains in power and resonance what it may lose in righteousness.

But in the United States, publishing any book of poems, as Ferlinghetti himself has said, is like rolling a boulder over a cliff. However heroic the effort, hardly anyone is likely to notice, and any response at all is a near miracle. Even his own latest, Northern California Book Award–winning epic poem, *Americus, Book I*, has not received the kind of critical attention routinely given to a new volume from John Ashbery or Jorie Graham or Robert Pinsky or Sharon Olds or any number of other well-known bards. Still, his stamina and consistency have brought on a blizzard of prizes and honors in the last few years—from the Author's Guild, the National Book Critics Circle, The ACLU, the Poetry Society of America, the American Academy of Arts and Letters, and most recently the National Book Awards. As one of the best-selling US poets ever, whose *A Coney Island of the Mind* has sold nearly a million copies in nine languages, he has managed to build a bridge between the high Modernism of T. S. Eliot and Ezra Pound and William Carlos Williams, and the popular appeal and easy access of Bruce Springsteen and John Lennon and Hank Williams.

I've always found Ferlinghetti's poems engaging and enjoyable, certainly more fully alive on the page than ninety percent of what's published in most magazines, but not especially compelling or profound in the sense of a vision that draws you deeper into its subtlety, strangeness or mystery. Almost everything is on the surface—it means exactly what it says—and that is no doubt part of its staying power with a great range of nonspecialist readers. His "Populist Manifesto" of the mid-1970s was a call to arms for poets to shun obscurity and to lay out language in a way that anyone can *get* it. "I saw the best minds of my generation destroyed by boredom at poetry readings" is a line that echoes endlessly in the psyches of those of us who know all too well what he's talking about. The great challenge is to make poems that are easily comprehensible and yet not prosaic or flat or cliché or pedestrian—poems that can walk and sing at the same time. Ferlinghetti's genius has been to sustain for over half a century the creative ingenuity to do just this, lifting the obvious into the extraordinary. Without taking himself too seriously, he engages the disturbed world with prophetic fervor, moving with a light step and a Whitmanic yawp through the dark truths of our time.

2006

Allen Ginsberg:
The Great Connector

Filing out of the synagogue at Temple Emanu-El in San Francisco following the memorial service for Allen Ginsberg, I turned to Jack Hirschman nearby in the aisle and said to him, "You know, Jack, it was in your class at UCLA that I first heard one of Allen Ginsberg's poems." Jack looked at me over his droopy mustache with his big inimitable grin and said, "That just shows how everything's connected."

In the spring of 1966, Ginsberg was almost forty and already a literary outlaw celebrity, "Howl" having been in print for a decade and firmly established in the countercanon. Hirschman was in his early thirties and a popular offbeat English professor on the Westwood campus, his Introduction to Poetry course consistently enrolled with at least two hundred students ranging from eagerly aspiring undergraduate poets to subliterate jocks in search of academic entertainment. I was a nineteen-year-old sophomore English major just getting acquainted with *The Norton Anthology* and trying to write my first immortal verses. Hirschman's official syllabus included *The Portable Walt Whitman, The Portable Blake* and Rilke's *Duino Elegies* (in the classic Leishman/Spender translation), but beyond those required texts it ranged from the *Tao Te Ching* and Japanese haiku through the Book of Genesis and "Lapis Lazuli" to Dr. Seuss and the "Sunflower Sutra." Ginsberg's language in that remarkable poem, mediated through Hirschman's electrifying presence, struck my dawning poetic consciousness with explosive force, simultaneously liberating and unsettling.

It was unsettling to me because I was still attempting to get a grip on the traditional conservative esthetic of English poesy. I wasn't yet ready to rebel against those somehow reassuring forms that I was just beginning to learn in earnest. Rhyme and meter were refuge and comfort for the emotional turmoil of adolescence. Yet here it was the mid-sixties, the war in Vietnam was getting more hellish daily, existential philosophy and the Beat revolt of the fifties were finally percolating into the cultural mainstream and it was obviously going to be impossible to avoid the disruptive impact of Ginsberg and his comrades. While many welcomed the Beat assault on literary law and order, I was too young and way too unhip to appreciate its revolutionary necessity.

That summer in England—England!—I picked up a pocket paperback volume of the Penguin Modern Poets series featuring Corso, Ferlinghetti and Ginsberg, and proceeded to study their exotic texts with more curiosity than understanding. By the time I started graduate school a little more than two years later—years of urban riots, political assassinations and escalating atrocities in Southeast Asia—I was ready to enlist my poetic gifts, such as they were, in the subversive forces, led by Ginsberg, whose mission was to overthrow the status quo by acts of angelic sabotage—like the 1967 March on Washington where the bearded bard conducted an exorcism and attempted to levitate the Pentagon.

Ginsberg's great documentary volumes of the next few years, *Planet News* (1968) and *The Fall of America* (1973), were inspirational beacons in dark times, poetry that necessarily escaped the limits of the merely literary and became a way of comprehending and responding to a historical moment gone over the far edge. It was in these tumultuous years—belatedly, I admit—that I truly grew to value the artistic genius and guerrilla courage of Ginsberg's cultural (anti-) leadership, his agitational identity as a model of creative resistance. In subsequent decades he became such a pervasive presence it was easy to take him for granted as a walking and talking monument to his own monumental ambition, his tremendous desire to be what he'd become, a freaky hybrid of Poet, Sage, Pundit, Rock Star, Clown, Teacher, Lover and Warrior. So that his sudden death April 5 left me, and thousands of others, unexpectedly shaken and bereft.

What more is there to say about Allen Ginsberg? After the blizzard of obituaries; after the reminiscences by his companions of the Beat era; after the commentaries by critics and the testimonies of his students; after the private conversations and grief-filled letters and phone calls and faxes and emails of those who, whether they knew him or not, felt his death as a deeply personal loss; and after his own preemptive autoerotic typically funny elegy for himself, "Death & Fame," in the pages of *The New Yorker*—a stroke of posthumous genius worthy of the master media-trickster he was—after all the boilerplate blather and the quotings from "Howl" and "Kaddish" and the remembrances by his million closest friends, is there really anything to add? Maybe not, but his contribution was on such a scale that it's impossible to stop talking about him. Which, as if he were directing an orgy of gossip from beyond the grave, is just as he would have wanted.

Poet and filmmaker Richard Moore recalled for me the moment in the mid-sixties when Ginsberg had won his first Guggenheim Fellowship and immediately invested some of the funds in a new Volkswagen camper. Moore and Ginsberg, with a film crew and "the great driver" and notorious speed freak Neal Cassady at the wheel, were tooling around San Francisco one day, Cassady careering up and down the hills as if he were racing a Ferrari. Ginsberg, ever the responsible one despite his reputation as a maniac, finally couldn't abide Cassady's reck-lessness and yelled, "Take it easy, I just got this thing!"

And here's another one you probably haven't heard, related to me by Fernando Alegría. Pablo Neruda had come to Berke-ley, circa 1971, to give a reading at Wheeler Hall on the UC campus, and Ginsberg was in attendance. According to Fer-nando, "Neruda was shy; he was afraid Ginsberg—which he pronounced Jinsberg—was going to do something wild. After the reading Ginsberg wanted to come with us to my house, where Neruda was staying. When Neruda saw Ginsberg approaching he said to me, 'Here comes Jinsberg, let's get out of here. You know, he likes to take off his clothes.'"

My personal recollections include a couple of encounters. At the Santa Cruz Poetry Festival, 1974, Ginsberg is onstage reading and is unexpectedly interrupted by one of the festival emcees coming out of the wings to whisper something in his ear. The poet returns to the mike and calmly announces to the fifteen hundred or so people packed into the Civic Auditorium that a bomb threat has been phoned in and the police require that the building be immediately evacuated. To facilitate the orderly clearing of the building Ginsberg proceeds to improvise a poem/incantation on the theme of the supposed bomb, cheerfully encouraging the exiting audience in spontaneously precise rhyme and measure, if we're going to die we'll do it together. As it turns out, no bomb is found, but the bard, all in a night's work, has composed a disposable emergency song for the occasion.

Santa Cruz again, circa 1982: walking with the poet's entourage to a local saloon for after-the-reading beers, I found myself alongside the recently clean-cut, suited-and-necktied Ginsberg and—a long-ago grad-school dropout myself—couldn't resist asking him how he liked being a college professor. "I love it," he replied without hesitation, "because I get to sleep with my students." It's hard to imagine any other poet, let alone academic, at that time candidly making such a declaration to someone he scarcely knew, but for Ginsberg candor (another aspect of that nakedness Neruda had worried about) was a way of life. He clearly saw himself not in the role of dirty old pervert or sexual predator but in the noble pedagogical tradition of Sappho and Socrates, teachers whose holistic instruction did not stop at the edge of the intellect but flowed naturally into every zone of experience.

This absence of inhibition—never mind that he was queer— is undoubtedly the reason Ginsberg was never appointed Poet Laureate by the Library of Congress despite the fact that he was uncontested as the preeminent National Poet of these States. More than Robert Frost or Maya Angelou, it was Ginsberg who should have been there to inaugurate presidents, and

I imagine if Jerry Brown had ever attained that office he would have had the good sense to name Ginsberg his inaugural bard. Appointing him to a Cabinet position or, say, Director of Central Intelligence might have been a bit more problematic, as his FBI file was no doubt enough to give any senator the shakes. The peripatetic poet may never have been a communist but at one time or another he was just about everything else hated and feared by the likes of Jesse Helms. Still, I can think of no other writer since Whitman more committed, in word and deed, to the democratic ideal. Ginsberg may have been a pot-smoking pill-popping mantra-chanting meditating cocksucking pedophilic anarcho-pacifist antinationalist renegade but he was also a great patriot, a mutant avatar of the American dream.

If Yeats, as Auden wrote, disappeared in the dead of winter, it's only right that Ginsberg should vanish as he did in early spring—in April, maybe not the cruelest but, more to the point, the foolish month, and National Poetry Month—with a spectacular comet ablaze in the night sky like an exclamation point, a comet called Hale-Bopp no less, as if in kabbalistic salute to Ginsberg's Kerouackian bop prosody and to his affinity with the Blakean proverb "He whose face gives no light will never become a star." All such signs and portents, such cosmic rhymes and shapely associations are classic Ginsbergian ingredients to stir into any posthumous soup or stew that one might wish to cook up in his memory.

A friend remembers Ginsberg in her kitchen preparing a meal, a telephone stuck to each ear, carrying on two conversations at once—counseling the mother of a former student in crisis out of one side of his mouth and doing business with his agent out of the other—all the while chopping garlic. Here we see the generously eclectic all-comforting all-consuming always hustling shaman/entrepreneur/healer/chef at work, steady of hand and mind, domestic and worldly, chaotic and organized, within and above it all at the same time. "I write poetry," he notes with characteristic self-contradiction in the Preface to *Cosmopolitan Greetings*, "because I want to be alone and want to talk to people." One can deduce that he used the telephone for similar purposes.

On a book tour for *Cosmopolitan Greetings* in the spring of 1994, Ginsberg appeared at Candlestick Park to read a poem and throw out the first ball for a Giants game before proceeding to more serious business at a local bookstore. Asked that night by a reporter for the *Chronicle*, "How does it feel for an iconoclast to have become an icon?" Ginsberg replied, "I consider myself a poet. Whether I'm an icon is somebody else's problem. I'm a coward and a jerk...like everybody else."

Like the published work of other prodigious anomalies, Ginsberg's voluminous art is vastly uneven, erratic, shaggy around the edges like his Uncle Sam persona of the sixties, full of intrinsic and extraneous nonsense, whatever-came-into-his-head, inspirational overload, an almost unforgivable excess of information. Yet it is precisely this open-to-everything inclusiveness—from spiritual revelations to international relations, from the devious dealings of the CIA to the state of his personal digestion—that makes him the emblematic chronicler of our time, the one who took responsibility for collecting the cultural garbage and attempting, with varying degrees of success, to recycle it through the imagination transformed as creative process—artistic or literary, political or revolutionary, religious or erotic, but always in a spirit of serious play. He gave himself, and by extension the rest of us, permission to be an idiot.

Whenever I'm writing badly, or have just made a fool of myself in public, or exposed some embarrassing private truth I ought to be ashamed of, I find consolation in the fact that Allen Ginsberg, bless his soul, was constantly doing these kinds of things only more so and far more famously, and with such evident purity of heart as to transcend all chagrin. That's why without even knowing him people feel as if they know him. Exceptional as he was in so many ways, he's also just like us—confused, imperfect, dopey, lonely, a typical human wreck—even as he maintains an equally honest and authentic dignity as scholar, diplomat, bodhisattva, philosopher, visionary, craftsman, rabbi. Just as his death became the occasion for a huge reunion of poets and friends and strangers from diverse communities and generations at the Temple Emanu-El gathering, his life in its very multiplicity shows how everything's connected.

1997

A Bard Is Born:
William Everson

While I have long respected William Everson's achievement and presence as a poet, I've never felt personally all that attuned to the poetry itself. The explicitly Christian thrust of much of his work (Everson had been a Dominican monk and went by the name of Brother Antoninus), the conscious echoes of Robinson Jeffers (a very hard bard to follow), and the strong thematic emphasis on masculine genital power have all contributed to my failure to feel fully at home in his verse. In 1976, however, when he published *Archetype West*, I began to discover a greater affinity with Everson's genius as a writer.

Archetype West is a daring experiment in literary history and theory—the kind of book which, in its range of insight and radical originality, leaves itself open to all sorts of academic objections. Everson's strength as a theoretician springs largely from his lack of critical credentials: writing as a poet rather than as a professor, he is able to speak from inside his subject ("the Pacific Coast as a Literary Region") with the authority of grounded intuition. *Archetype West* gave me a fresh and useful understanding of what it means to live and write in California.

As an interpretation of West Coast culture, it's a major contribution to our collective sense of identity.

For a dozen years now, Everson has served as poet-in-residence at UCSC's Kresge College, teaching an unconventional course called Birth of a Poet. Far from your standard undergraduate introduction-to-poetry class, Birth of a Poet explores the poet's *vocation* by way of a loosely structured series of spontaneous talks in which Everson meditates on his personal creative evolution. A year's worth of these meditations (recorded in 1975–76 and edited by Lee Bartlett) has recently been issued by Black Sparrow Press. *Birth of a Poet* lets us listen in on the musings of a remarkable mind in the process of examining what it means to be an artist.

Everson's erudition is considerable but these reflections are far from bookish. Focusing first on the spiritual/religious aspects of the poet's calling, he gradually finds his way round to the historic and geographic factors at work in his own (and, by extension, anyone's) development. The intensely personal nature of his discoveries leaves plenty of room for disagreement—Everson is unapologetically subjective in outlook—but that very intensity gives his voice a resonance which sounds to me like wisdom.

It isn't knowledge but *meaning* that the teacher is trying to impart in *Birth of a Poet*. Everson is concerned with the fundamental question of how to live a meaningful life in a time with very few reliable guidelines. We hear a man in his middle sixties relating to a roomful of twenty-year-olds the insights of a lifetime, admonishing them to engage the myths of their individual destinies, to be aware of their dreams, to plant themselves in the landscapes where they belong, to come to terms with their culture as a means of knowing themselves. Through aphorisms, jokes, poems, anecdotes, historical analysis, philosophical associations, lyrical reveries—all brief and lucid and subtly inter-connected—Everson weaves a network of reference which his students (and readers) may take or leave but won't easily be able to ignore.

Our lives depend on such references as Everson has to offer—even when we don't wholly accept them—because each person, in the light of myth, is the hero of his or her particular epic. To recognize the mythic significance of one's personal saga presents the risk of narcissistic self-consciousness and all its attendant ego problems, but it also opens the prospect of entering into communal life with something substantial to contribute.

Such a mythic undertaking can't be realized in a vacuum. Carefully setting his sense of the individual in the context of collective experience—American history, the Western landscape, interpersonal relations—Everson tries to make us aware of *where* as well as who we are and what we may become. The role of the terrain we inhabit, its textures and contours and rhythms, is just as crucial to our growth as the people we interact with or the books we read. Much more than merely a literary pursuit, poetry is a way of participating in and helping to shape reality.

"A great poem," wrote Whitman, "is no finish to a man or woman but rather a beginning." *Birth of a Poet* is a point of departure for those who wish to investigate the values Everson has brought from the source. More than Jeffers, I dare say more than Jesus, Whitman's presence informs his approach to the practice of the poet's profession. Everson speaks in these "Santa Cruz Meditations" out of an inexhaustible tradition which the author of *Song of Myself* embodied: the poet as human art moving in the world. For the shaman/bard, as Everson conceives him, public self-revelation is a form of prayer. And song, drawn from the depths of one's soul, can be a form of salvation.

1982

Bob Kaufman's
Long Goodbye

The same January afternoon that Omar Cabezas was in the city, Bob Kaufman's ashes were scattered over San Francisco Bay. The ceremony followed a movable wake that snaked through the streets of North Beach saying goodbye to the legendary poet who'd perished a few days earlier. As Cabezas signed copies of his memoir of the Sandinista revolution in Lawrence Ferlinghetti's City Lights Books, video cameras and flashguns blazing among the wine-tasters, poets who'd just said so-long to Kaufman came wandering in off Columbus Avenue to salute the author of Nicaragua's all-time best-selling book (published in the US, in Kathleen Weaver's translation, as *Fire from the Mountain*). Cabezas, renowned throughout Latin America for his lively style as a storyteller, had come to the States as a guest of the PEN International Congress in New York. Kaufman, the defeated beatnik, had helped revolutionize American poetry some thirty years earlier but died in a state of literary obscurity. As I stood in City Lights observing the interplay of poets and press and hangers-around, I mused on the ironies of the scene.

America, whose revolutionary history continually recurs in Kaufman's poems with a tragicomic sparkle of celebration, may have rejected his weird and lyrical contribution to the sprawling body of the nation's letters—his work was better known in Europe than in the States—but in the relative intimacy of the neighborhood he haunted for many years his staggering, raving presence was well established. The divine madness so desperately sought by so many bardic charlatans was embodied in Kaufman with painful reality. That he lived to be sixty, under the burden of his evident distress, is almost a miracle in itself. Accounts of his life resound with echoes of tragically bad luck, collisions with the police, time behind bars, electro-shock "therapy," drug addiction, alcoholism, racial discrimination (his parents were German Jewish and Afro-Caribbean in origin) and various other curses of the crazed or nonconforming artist. When President Kennedy was assassinated, Kaufman took a vow of silence, publishing nothing and scarcely speaking for ten full years. As he faded away during the last decade, his body destroyed by sidewalk life and substance abuse, his genius reportedly flared at times in lucid moments of spoken poesy, but he was a dazed remnant of whatever he'd been before—a ghost of poetry past, a deranged angel.

The irony of Kaufman's funeral falling on the day Cabezas came to his neighborhood is striking. Cabezas, a wiry thirty-five, former guerrilla fighter, revolutionary commander in Nicaragua's Interior Ministry, is a famous author not because of any literary ambition but due to his natural talent for spinning tales. As an exponent of testimony rather than fiction, he confessed to relying more on his own experience than on any knowledge of the masterworks of Latin American writing. "In

Nicaragua there's a saying," he told the press, "that everybody's a poet unless proved otherwise." While Nicaraguan writers are free to cultivate alienation if so inclined—and while some of that country's poets may be drunks or otherwise demented types—there's clearly a place of honor in the culture for those who practice the art of national hero and pioneer Modernist Rubén Darío. Poetry in Nicaragua, both amateur and professional, is almost as popular a pastime as baseball. The Ministry of Culture has institutionalized writing workshops around the country. Well-known writers and poets occupy important positions in the government. All three major papers publish weekly literary supplements. Creativity is emphasized as a key element in revolutionary change. Among the equipment young Sandinista soldiers take to the front in the *contra* war is a notebook in which they're encouraged to record their thoughts and exercise their imaginations. The minimal tolerance or veiled contempt reserved for poets in the United States is a condition with which Nicaraguans are unfamiliar.

This is not necessarily to say that Bob Kaufman would have been better off in Nicaragua, nor that most of the poets in North America should be signing up for political appointments; it is merely to observe with curiosity that our "freedom of speech"–loving country should so ignore its creative voices while the allegedly repressive Sandinistas actively cultivate theirs. Cabezas, the nonwriter who speaks his works into a tape recorder, is—like many of his more literary *compañeros*—an active shaper of his country's identity, both cultural and political, and as such enjoys a professional dignity seldom accorded US writers, least of all the offbeat likes of Kaufman.

But Kaufman's persona, informed by a deeply authentic

grief and seemingly lifelong pain, reflected the kind of relentless suffering that some would-be geniuses believe to be essential to their art. Numerous hard-drinking, drug-taking, imagery-slinging idiots in search of Rimbaudelairean revelations have littered the bohemian backwaters of our cities with utterly forgettable poetic drivel while pretending to exquisite immortality and berating the powers that be for not paying more attention to their smoke-stained, wine-soaked, beer-breath'd, pill-fried, semi-psychotic utterances. These bards playing the game of the star-crossed Keatsnik or Beat Romantic tragically ignored by the Philistines are no more pathetic, really, than the well-groomed suburban workshop graduates who publish their instant nostalgic odes in academic journals, but somehow all such poses are beside the point. It's worth remembering that the major survivors of the Beat movement (Allen Ginsberg, Gary Snyder, Michael McClure, Philip Whalen and Ferlinghetti, to name the most obvious ones whose presence has been felt in California) have gone on to cultivate healing, holistic visions to replace the alienation they may have felt as freaks in the 1950s. It is this wholeness I'd like to see more of in the writings and lives of my contemporaries and the generations coming up behind us.

Despite the rampant boredom of so much magazine verse being published now, and notwithstanding the conservative waves of neoconformity washing out the spirits of computerized Yankee youth, I detect a few vital signs that suggest we may be in for some sort of realistic visionary renewal. Just as New York and San Francisco painters and poets of the fifties and sixties inspired artists and writers everywhere with their daring explorations of form and feeling—not to mention the monster jazz musicians whose sounds were heard and felt in the hearts of hipsters the world over—waves of insight and inspiration are returning to these shores from places scarcely known here in those years. Looking almost exclusively to Europe for artistic models, most of the hottest cookers of US culture neglected to notice resources closer to home which now appear to be having a major impact. From Latin America we've heard new voices that have upset conventional expectations easily as much as the Beats did in their day. Young North American Latinos especially have picked up the energies of our hemispheric neighbors and are deep in the process of creating hybrid texts and songs and stories that blend the rhythms and traditions of both continents. This may be more visible now in California and parts of the Southwest, but inevitably it will be felt much farther afield.

The work of poets in the coming years seems less likely to confine itself to the ghetto in which it has languished these recent decades, nor does it need to be limited to the pages of obscure journals. Verse itself may be a dying species—its withering corpses in most of their current forms would not be missed—but the inventive juices and practical commitment that keep poems and writers alive can be found in the conduct of people devoted to creating a world where imagination matters. How this imagination manifests itself is one of the mysteries I look forward to witnessing as the moon sets on this century. The angelic genius of Kaufman, liberated from his tortured life, is honored by those who refuse to succumb to the sorrow and despair that drove him under. The tenderness and humor of his poetry—kept alive by the likes of Cabezas and others recording with care and consciousness the victories of the spirit—will easily outlast his lonely solitude.

"I look down on the Earth and see myself wandering in the Ancient Rain," wrote Kaufman in one of his last known poems. I'm told that as his ashes were strewn to the wind an enormous rainbow appeared over the Golden Gate.

1986

Gary Snyder's
Common Knowledge

A quiet Sunday in Soquel Valley, wisps of white cloud high over-head; jays and woodpeckers screech and chatter in nearby trees while a neighbor's radio blares the World Series—the Orioles are winning—and he works on his place, getting ready for rain. I'm reading Gary Snyder's new book, *Axe Handles*, absorbing background sounds of chainsaws, birds and baseball.

Snyder's writing brings you alive to where you are, opens the senses to present subtleties, unburies the obvious. I taste cold water pumped from local ground, feeling its iron in my teeth, and am reminded it flows here underground out of the Sierras. Oak in the stove came down in last year's storms, warms the house now, perfumes and pollutes the air.

Between innings, commercials echoing from my neighbor's ghetto-blaster bring the more blatant idiocies of civilization painfully into the picture—just as in Snyder's poems fighter planes and logging trucks intrude on his loving attention to the natural textures of the land. The poet's awareness is wiry enough to hold these realms in tension, acknowledging "the pain / of the work / of wrecking the world" without succumbing to it. It's rather the "relentless clarity / at the heart / of work" that counts.

Axe Handles is a book distilled from years of homesteading in the Sierra foothills; traveling as far as Sweden, Japan, Australia, Alaska and Sacramento; working as an administrator in California cultural politics; raising two sons and passing knowledge and know-how along to them. The voice is calm, clear, readily accessible to any attentive ear. Poems, too, are tools—recipes, incantations, songs of praise, stones for sharpening the mind.

It's been about thirty years since Snyder's poetry began to emerge in public. He was among the original "Beats" whose appearance in San Francisco in the 1950s opened American literature to fresh and fertile possibilities. But the dominant strain of that movement—most famously embodied in such writers as Allen Ginsberg and Jack Kerouac—while certainly dynamic and powerful in its way, seems to have been corrupted in the process of its transmission—corrupted by booze and drugs, the junk of popular consciousness, by electricity, internal combustion and other funky realities of urban bohemia.

Many of Snyder's finest poems are set in and around San Francisco, addressing the delicious complexities of city life, its pleasures and poisons, transforming the concrete, cars and sewage, neon, plastic and propaganda into the most invigorating music. But his years of study in Japan, his deep explorations of Asian and Native American cultures, his intelligent wanderings over the wilderness of the western United States, and more recently his experience as a family man and farmer, have given his vision a kind of coherence and physical wisdom absent from the work of many of his contemporaries.

One thing that gives Snyder's writing its character is that he knows how to do a lot more than just write. Poetry may be "the eagle of experience" but unless the bird has been nurtured on other practical sources it isn't likely to fly.

In my opinion, Snyder's most exciting books date from the 1960s—*The Back Country, Six Sections* (from *Mountains and Rivers Without End*) and *Regarding Wave*—before he was made officially respectable by the 1975 Pulitzer Prize for *Turtle Island*. The environmental message in that volume was certainly important, but the restless quickness of thought, precision of observation and range of consciousness in so many of the earlier poems keep them as fresh and vigorous today as ever.

Still, all the living he has done since then gives his more recent work a sinewy root system that reaches beyond the poems. *Axe Handles,* perhaps *because* it is not quite as challenging as the earlier books in terms of language and speed of association, may touch those people less inclined to tackle more difficult texts. For many, Snyder's presence in the last ten years or so has become easily as important as his poetry. Like his friend Wendell Berry and others who have grown into "the old ways" of working the earth as a healthy long-range mode of survival in harmony with the rest of creation, Snyder has become a model of a certain kind of integrity, and as such means more to a public hungry for functional alternatives than he ever did as a strictly "literary" figure.

How much his popularity as an organic guru matters to him or his art, I'm not too sure. But I believe his visibility in what William Everson would call a "charismatic" role has clearly proposed a way of being in the world which many people are richer for knowing about, even if they're not all able to find their own land to work. The principles of respect for the earth and for one's human and natural communities apply to city dwellers as well as to country folk.

Snyder's value to the rest of us is less a matter of "lifestyle"—of someone to imitate in dress or haircut or brand of hiking boots—than of imagination and moral values. Going over his writings from the beginning, one sees a graceful arc of creative growth which has remained amazingly true to its own eccentric yet down-to-earth purposes and pattern. Living responsibly, with vivid presence of mind, is what his poetry is all about.

1983

Lyrical Politics:
The Art of **Jack Hirschman**

I and mine do not convince by arguments, similes, rhymes;
We convince by our presence.

WALT WHITMAN, "Song of the Open Road"

Jack Hirschman was the first poet I ever met.

Early 1966: I had just turned nineteen and was studying "English" at UCLA while engaged in my first serious mixups with the muses. Adolescence, the early sparks of intellect, the expanding specter of the war in Vietnam, impossible conflicts with the dominant values surrounding me at home in my folks' house and fear of the social alternatives—all turned me deeper into poetry as a life-support system.

But most of the poets I knew of, or felt I could gain any useful guidance from, were either premature Monuments (like Auden and Dylan Thomas) or had been dead for at least a century. Poetry was something in books (as "art" was something in museums and on well-heeled walls; decorative, beautiful even, but old and overpriced), not a vital activity one could *do* in the open, much less professionally. People like Keats and Coleridge were poets—marginal characters at best—and most contemporary free-versers were not just temporary but incomprehensible too. Maybe my mother was right: poetry was permissible, but only "on the side."

Meanwhile in Westwood, Hirschman, a brilliant young renegade professor, was giving a course called Introduction to Poetry. Already semi-legendary for his eccentric teaching style, "Mad Jack" (or "Dr. Hirschman," depending on whose projection you subscribed to) was rumored to be an inspired and inspiring character. As it turned out, attending that class—one of the last he was to offer as even a borderline academic—was a decisive step in my education, and I bet the same could be said for many of his students at that time. As one of some two hundred taking the course, my direct contact with the professor was minimal; in fact, what little comment I received from him on my own writing was hardly encouraging. Among other things the literary formalism with which I was trying to train myself as a writer cut backward across the extemporaneous synchronicity Hirschman was expounding.

But he certainly encouraged dialogue and the practice of poetry among those present; Fridays were set aside for the weekly "haiku contest" which eventually developed into full-scale readings and festive rituals that were often exhilarating. His reading recommendations ranged from Dostoyevsky to Dr. Seuss, the *Tao Te Ching* to the Book of Genesis, not to mention the assigned texts: Whitman, Blake, and Rilke's *Duino Elegies*. And he incited to write: the term assignment was to keep a notebook. Still more disturbing to the English major, he challenged every currently respectable assumption as to poetry's composition and its study.

His presence—a nervous/chain-smoking combination of energy, lucidity and cryptic charismania pervaded by a contagious lyrical enthusiasm—exemplified, *embodied* a wild side of the art which *The Norton Anthology* never acknowledged. Without inviting imitators or disciples (in fact discouraging hero worship of any sort as founded on vanity, fantasy and false impressions), Hirschman's bearing bespoke the possibilities— the hazards too—of poetry. Like no other person I'd ever met, he showed the spirit in revolution struggling to rupture the rigid structures of the status quo.

Surely Jack himself would be the first to protest such "studential" invocations of "our dead brains" of those days, preferring fellow poets to regard him as a comrade, not a teacher. Yet the same incorrigible radicalism that got him kicked out of academia—his opposition to the Vietnam War led him to give A's to all his male students as a way of helping them avoid the draft—remains an essential aspect of his subsequent commitment. The highly idiosyncratic brand of romantic "communism" Hirschman has practiced over the years in the streets and cafés of San Francisco has made him no less controversial a figure in the California poetry community than he ever was on campus. If his prodigious and at times bewildering overflow of poems, translations, editorial activities and artwork have given him a certain tenure as a force in the literary/political networks of the West Coast, the intensity of his convictions and the openness with which he manifests them—flamboyantly writing and reciting in public places, for example, raving against the delusions of electronics, or loudly espousing solidarity in the face of fascism—have also aroused in some a skepticism bordering on incredulousness.

Because his poetry does not yield to conventional critical analysis nor to the self-congratulatory rhetoric-and-response of less imaginative freedom fighters (much less to personalistic demands that the poet confess everything in an orgy of self-justification), Hirschman's published writings alone do not convey his full powers as a poet. His handwriting itself (for years he's avoided typewriters) is idiogrammatical, the expressive energy in his puns and penstrokes extremely rambunctious—charged—and the shapes of lines on the page forceful/graceful, "projective" in functional visual design based on the human breath. Each poem is a handwrought document, paradoxically disposable, one of a kind, not meant to be reproduced except by the voice, by the exponential powers of collective imagination. Often of course they are reproduced—in broadsides, magazines and more than thirty books to date—each text to be regarded as a musical score for the reader's inner ear.

For if Hirschman is a calligraffiti-fingerpainter and murrealist-without-walls he's also an oral/aural poet: he speaks in the bloodlines of the street corner, the jazz singer, the shaman-buffoon, using his considerable erudition and passionate grasp of a wealth of arcane and common information to transform his anguished exuberance into music—real mouth-and-diaphragm music to be sounded aloud in public among fellow citizens, or intimately to comrade/friend and lover. Poems of his that may not seem to get off the page in print can come alive in his performance of them in ways one never anticipated—without the use of props or gimmicks currently popular in some poetry/showbiz circles (bards with autoharps, jews harps, blues harps, etc.)—at times approaching schizophrenese in their subtle dissociations of sense and syntax—complex incantations unraveling phrase by rhythmic phrase, or coming straight to the point, simply—yet coming across, voiced, as a moving and unmistakably Hirschmanic mixture of Joyce and bebop-kabbalism and praise and propagan*duende*.

Spraying fine spit indiscreetly into the front rows as he reads, Hirschman live reveals as in a seizure his visionary authenticity: his voice has heroism in it, is vigorous, because he inhabits his work as an ongoing vocation, a long-term revolutionary spiritual assignment.

As he notes in front of his recent collection *Lyripol* (City Lights, 1976), "I know *in fact* that every poem which follows was written by innumerable comrades who came through the skins of my translations and graphic scrawls and, in the highest form of mass creation (an extended situation that has included street-school-farm-prison), urged these works from me as communist creations through the particular, romantic and even esoteric habits I practice daily."

Taking dictation from the quotidian romance acoustically transmused through his own lungs and tongue and given back freely, unrepeatably, into the improvisational consciousness stream from which it came, Hirschman enacts rites on behalf of all who would be moved. In their "Manifestation" of *AMERUS, a multilingual lyripolitical journal of poetry and graphics* uniting America and Russia in an amorous embrace (Amerus Press, 1979), he and coeditor Alexander Kohav echo the Surrealists' assertion that "Works of art should be considered as news items." Yet they insist: "We are not another stage of surrealism. We are not media flunkies of a persistent chemical mysticism. The hired 'free-expressionism' of abstracted control rooms—anywhere in the world—isn't our idea of a poet's job. The blue milk of Da-Da, since it cowtows to a Nyet-Nyet trippy video or a four-facetted jerusabuddhism, isn't our journey. The journal presented here is a passport to sanity in terms of national schizophrenias." Poetry is political by nature to the degree that artist and audience inter-exchange meaningful language as an alternative to money. Uncompromising creative intuition is a liberator.

Lived existentially as Hirschman lives them, such seemingly "idealistic" principles take on a most convincing concreteness. What may appear to the competitive as ego-tripping is more often an incredible generosity. If his agitpropulsion repels some people, he is also respected for conducting occult gifts into public light. This power is most obviously displayed in his prolific work as a translator (from at least a half dozen languages). The speakable North American idiom in which he renders numerous little-known foreign poets—not to mention his frontline work on Artaud, Mayakovsky, Neruda, Eluard and other major writers—is a risky but invaluable model of translation as re-creation. The occasional liberties or mistakes the meticulous may detect and disapprove of are due largely to the speed and spontaneity, the high metabolic rate at which he works. But compare Hirschman's translations to those of most of his colleagues and see which come out sounding more like poetry. Consistently his attunement to the extraordinary flexibilities of common American English reminds one of the richness still alive in our battered vernacular.

Combining the cool savvy of a gypsy scholar with the inner fire of a guerrilla, a fool's shrewdness with the earthiness of a shoemaker, Jack Hirschman lives and works with an integrity which transcends as it suffuses the surface of his personality.

He is a poet of the heart and is keeping alive an agitator/troubadour tradition synthesized in his mind multilingually from many cultures, a humane international/planetary tradition of resistance, transformation and communion.

1980

Bukowski:
The Long View

1 Dirty Old Master

Whatever else you can say about Charles Bukowski, there's no denying his endurance. Revered by many as anti-literary hero, reviled by others as an affront to decency, regarded by still others as an amusing but negligible underground eccentric, Bukowski at seventy continues to document his days and nights with a seemingly unstoppable flow of poems and stories that have firmly established him as a survivor in the international literary landscape. His informal, conversational, nasty yet crafty style as a poet has influenced, for better and worse, two or three generations of younger writers. The prose of his novels has grown clearer and sharper even as the tone has become kindlier. The sheer volume and diversity of his output—thirty-five books in thirty years—makes him something of a poor man's answer to Joyce Carol Oates.

But Bukowski is poor no more. Sales of his books in the US and abroad have long since turned him into a comfortable homeowner and BMW driver (and, as a recent poem reports, American Express Gold Card carrier) who commutes to the racetrack with classical music on the car stereo and drinks French wine instead of steering his wreck to dead-end jobs and guzzling cheap booze. And he keeps on, publishing three books since 1988: *The Roominghouse Madrigals*, a selection of early poems previously uncollected or out of print; *Hollywood*, a novel based on his experiences with director Barbet Schroeder making the movie *Barfly*; and *Septuagenarian Stew*, an assortment of more recent stories and poems. As if to cap the author's successful arrival at venerability, Random House last year brought out Neeli Cherkovski's *Hank: The Life of Charles Bukowski*, "the first biography written with Bukowski's full cooperation," says the flap copy, apparently signaling that New York's literary-industrial complex—of which Random is a major corporate cornerstone—has finally acknowledged his importance.

It's worthwhile to consider just what it is that has earned this writer such a large and devoted readership. Initially emerging in the magazines of the mimeo explosion of the 1960s, Bukowski's poems revealed him as a rough and original voice aligned with none of the prevailing schools or movements, a voice whose vulgarity and clarity and humor were startlingly unique. His work seemed to show up everywhere, soon attracting wide attention throughout the underground grapevine. His evident ease of expression had been earned over four decades of difficulties that would have killed most people, or at least crushed the poetry out of them. Raised in Los Angeles in the 1920s and 1930s by a brutally abusive father and a meek German-immigrant mother, the young Henry Charles Bukowski Jr. suffered social ostracism as a child, a hideous case of acne as an adolescent and chronic alcoholism as an adult. He took various jobs, bummed around, drank continuously, went in and out of jails, trying meanwhile to write short stories and sending them unsuccessfully to magazines. In 1955 he was hospitalized with a bleeding ulcer. One of his doctors told him he was a dead man if he took another drink. When he got out he resumed drinking but he also started writing poetry. The latter somehow seems to have worked as an antidote to the former, and since the age of thirty-five Bukowski has been steadily doing both.

In 1967 his weekly column "Notes of a Dirty Old Man" began appearing in *Open City*, a Los Angeles underground newspaper of the day, and later in the LA *Free Press*. While developing his prose style in the short form of the column, Bukowski was also vastly expanding his audience from the limited network of the little presses to a general if "alternative" readership. Independent publisher John Martin discovered him around the same time, and Martin's Black Sparrow Press began bringing out his books, which continue to be a mainstay of that operation. Profits from sales of Bukowski have helped keep alive one of the most reputable small publishers in the business, enabling Black Sparrow to bring into print the work of many less-celebrated writers.

The tale of Bukowski's climb from the gutter to glamour would be almost romantic if not for the crummy details recorded along the way by the author's unflinching eye. Rather than portray himself as a hero in his autobiographical saga, Bukowski bares himself, scars and all, as an unsavory everyman who nevertheless notices a lot of what's going on around him and renders it in language anyone can understand. He is an anti-poet obsessed with senselessness and cruelty and decay and death yet also on the alert for tiny moments of redeeming joy that surface when you least expect them, "the click of miracle," when the sunlight falls on the jockeys' silks just so, or the cat looks at you in a certain way.

Even in *The Roominghouse Madrigals*, poems written during his hardest years, there is a lyric impulse in Bukowski's language that reaches through its misery for transcendence:

> sterile faces squeezed out from squalid tubes of
> bodies ream and blind me to any
> compromise.
> I would crawl down into the black volcanic gut of a
> chicken and
> hide hide hide.
> listen, I know you think I am bitter and
> maybe insane, well
> that's all right
> but find me a place...

In another poem entitled "I Don't Need a Bedsheet with Slits for Eyes to Kill You in," the poet declares in a vicious echo of Carl Sandburg tinged with shades of Faulkner:

> if the fog comes in like soft cleanser
> and you can see old men looking out at it
> from behind curtains
> these warm old men smoking pipes
> I will tell you stories to make your dreams
> easier;
> but if you mutilate me
> hang me alongside the scarecrow like a
> cheap Christ

and let some schoolboy hang a sign about my
throat
I'm going to walk your streets of night
with a knife…
and when I decide finally that we will
meet
you will not understand
because you did not want
to
and the flowers and the dogs and the
cities and the children will not
miss you.

These poems display the rage and agony of the outcast, or more accurately, as Cherkovski notes, the outsider, the self-exiled misfit who has assumed the role of loser with a mixture of resignation, dignity, irony and defiance. It is the voice of the "lone nut," the ruined individual, the homeless person one can see any day on the streets of virtually every American city. But it is also an existential voice, speaking from beyond alienation, a voice affirming itself through the act of writing and thereby summoning the courage to carry on.

Not that the writer has any inside track on reality; as Bukowski informs us in another poem, writers

…are the most sickening
of all the louts!
yellow-toothed, slump-shouldered,
gutless, flea-bitten and
obvious…in tinker-toy rooms

> with their flabby hearts
> they tell us
> what's wrong with the world—
> as if we didn't know that a cop's club
> can crack the head
> and that war is a dirtier game than
> marriage…

He doesn't exclude himself from this judgment, honestly assessing the vanity of trying to change the world with words. The most one can hope for is to talk back at bad luck, make it give a little, ease up on the pressure. At worst such bleak defeatism results in the blubbering bathos of the drunk, but Bukowski's tough-guy posture and comic self-awareness give him the strength to go on building, word by word, a cumulative body of evidence that he's anything but defeated.

In a story called "Action" in *Septuagenarian Stew* he scans the patrons at the racetrack:

> Most of the people didn't look too happy. There were many Mexicans and blacks in the crowd, hoping to score, hoping to break their chains. They never would. They were only adding more links to their chains. The whites seemed most pitiful, flabby, with their deadly angry eyes. Most were male. One thing about the white male, though, he was wonderful material for the writer. You could write anything you wanted to about the white American male and nobody ever protested. Not even the white American male. But if you wrote anything disagreeable about any other race or class

or gender the critics and the public became furious and your hate mail stacked up, although book sales didn't seem to drop off. When they hated you, they had to read you. They were aching to see what you would say next about their world. While the white American male didn't give a damn what you said about him because he ruled the world—at the moment, anyhow.

There's a complexity of perception at work here that encompasses both identification with these pitiful pale creatures and mockery of their predicament, both a humorous contempt for those who scream racism or sexism whenever they get the chance and an ironic gratitude for these critics' attention. The writer also shows a sly understanding of the tenuousness of the sociopolitical status quo.

Which is not to suggest that Bukowski is a political writer. It doesn't matter to him who rules the world or is run over by it, they're all fair game, nobody's innocent. As Cherkovski points out, he has consistently rejected the notion of the writer as social reformer or activist. Bukowski finds consolation for the common disappointments in a few reliable companions: the horses, classical music, the bottle and the typewriter, a combination of elements that recur continuously, especially in the more recent work. As might be expected, this somewhat limited sphere of reference tends to dilute through repetition the power of some of his later collections. Still, frequently enough the vision crystallizes in a perfect poem or story. His goal as an artist is clearly not to make a flawless artifact but to document a life in all its contradictory ugliness and grace. Like

Robinson Jeffers, another California recluse whom Cherkovski identifies as a forebear, Bukowski is not attempting to please the crowd. His words on Jeffers in *Stew* reflect an aspect of his own integrity:

> his voice was dark
> a rock-slab pronouncement
> a voice not distracted by
> the ordinary forces of
> greed, cunning and
> need
>
> he was on a hunt
> listening to life

In these later poems Bukowski's style is leaner, flatter, more linear, more narrative than in the *Madrigals*, but the flatness itself has a certain relentless force.

As age and prosperity have caught up with him, Bukowski has sweetened a little—evidently with help from his wife of the last several years, Linda Lee Beighle, who has improved his eating and drinking habits—and his work since the mid-1980s has assumed a warmer tone, dwelling as much on the everyday pleasures of his middle-class life in LA's South Bay suburbs as on the nightmares of his urban past. He is obviously grateful for having survived all those earlier horrors, yet hasn't abandoned the crustiness of his outlook, combing his memory for revealing moments of illumination, relishing the routines of the present and invoking the friendship of the great dead in whose traditions he sees himself: Li Po, Celine, John Fante. In a poem called "drunk with the Buddha" he writes:

there is this small Buddha
he
sits on the desk
across from me and he
appears to be
laughing at
me.

I attempt to read
him: it seems as if he was saying:
our limitations are our
strengths.
let
everything else
go.

This has been Bukowski's strategy from the beginning, cultivating his limitations and, even with his recent success, resisting the illusions of celebrity, refusing to play the role of the distinguished writer, opting instead for drunken solitary laughter.

And yet it is those famous illusions that are so entertainingly portrayed in the novel *Hollywood*. While it lacks the urgency, intensity and anguish of his earlier novels *Post Office, Factotum, Women* and *Ham on Rye, Hollywood* is an easygoing and bemused account of the author's adventures in the motion-picture business. It should be noted that Bukowski is a local writer in the best sense of the term, rooted in his Los Angeles turf and endlessly unearthing its indigenous reality without ever pretending to speak as a public voice. Throughout his works he has mapped the nervous energy of LA's streets, its automotive obsessions, its architectural pathos, the truly mundane and unglamorous side of its media-warped facade. In *Women* especially one gets the sense of frenetic desperation that permeates the city. But because he grew up in Los Angeles and knows its people—its postal workers and skid-row winos and down-at-the-heels residents of shabby courts—his portrayal of the city and its inhabitants lacks the bitterness and contempt so often found in the writings of newcomers taking a fantasy-shattering peek into the dream factory.

In *Hollywood* Bukowski has a long look at the flashier side of LA, its producers and directors and actors and other toilers and hustlers in the Industry, and exercises a wise restraint in his judgments. After witnessing a tantrum by Jack Bledsoe, the young star of the film he has written, Bukowski's alter-author Henry Chinaski tries to make sense of the actor's behavior:

> I just decided that actors were different than we were. They had their own reasons for things. You know, when you spend many hours, many years pretending to be a person who you aren't, well, that can do something to you. It's hard enough just trying to be yourself. Think of trying very hard to be somebody that you're not. And then being somebody *else* that you're not. And then somebody else. At first, you know, it could be exciting. But after a while, after being dozens of other people, maybe it would be hard to remember who you were yourself, especially if you had to make up your own lines.

A younger Chinaski/Bukowski might have ripped into the pretense of the star mentality, shredding the veil of arrogance to show the vacancy and vanity that drives such deluded egos. Instead, he gently attempts to analyze the nature of the syndrome. This good-humored perspective on the follies of showbiz gives *Hollywood* a lightness of touch absent not only from most of his earlier writing but also from that of most other authors outraged and exasperated by their encounters with the film industry's trappings. Bukowski's no-fault vision of Hollywood is a genial complement to Nathanael West's horrific take in *The Day of the Locust* fifty years before.

Beyond being a book about the movies, *Hollywood* is, like *Stew*, a relaxed and confident account of the coming of age. It is a self-portrait of someone comfortable with his own durability yet constantly conscious of impending death. This sense of inevitable oblivion may be what gives the book its sweetness. The bite is gone, the writing is less exciting as the anguish has subsided, but there's an earned wisdom and self-assurance that show a fairly contented old fart telling his story for the pleasure of it. It is, after all, the only life he's got.

1991

2 Clean Old Man

The photo in back of Charles Bukowski's latest collection of poems—a four-hundred-page tome turned out as the author was approaching and passing seventy—shows a face seasoned by pain and suffering into an expression of tough equanimity, of weary compassion for the human dilemma. It is a face facing up to its own mortality: wise, gentle, kind. As anyone who's read his recent work is aware, Bukowski has lately lost his edge of angst; his comic meanness has sweetened into a humbly ironic gratitude for survival. The voice of the vicious drunk, while still vulgar in its raw directness, has taken on a far more philosophical tone, an attitude of acceptance if not quite understanding. Despite the spiky white whiskers grizzling his chin in the picture, his shirt collar is crisply pressed, his fingernails look immaculate: the once disreputable poet/bum as clean old man.

Comfortably ensconced as a homeowner in middle-class San Pedro, chatting across the backyard fence with his neighbors, driving his BMW on the freeways, using his credit cards to cash in on his international success, Bukowski has come a long way from the squalid urban landscape of his formative years in Los Angeles. Readers who dismissed his earlier writing as crude and monotonous are unlikely to find much to admire in the mellower, more prosaic lines of his latest work. And those who loved the wildly anti-literary beast desperately flailing at life's cruelties with flights of salty imagination may be disappointed to find the irascible bard gone soft. But those who have watched in wonder as he has brought forth book after book in an unstoppable flow of personal testimony since the early 1960s will find in this new volume further evidence not only of the man's astounding perseverance but of something approaching greatness.

It's not just that Bukowski's best poetry and prose—in books like *The Days Run Away Like Wild Horses Over the Hills* (1969), *Mockingbird Wish Me Luck* (1972), *Love Is a Dog From Hell* (1977), *War All the Time* (1984) and the novels *Women*

(1978) and *Ham on Rye* (1982)—have such a distinctive clarity, music and courage in their transformation of terrible experience; it is the cumulative proof the writer has provided that even the most apparently hopeless life can be converted to something useful, not only to the self but to others, through the effort of art.

The poems in *The Last Night of the Earth Poems* tend to be typically straight-ahead narratives, little stories both sad and funny, extended meditations laced with aphoristic kickers, accounts of mundane events that in the telling take on a certain matter-of-fact resonance, philosophical reflections on a past that won't go away. While the present may afford him the material luxuries of drinking expensive wine and working on a new computer, the old days at pointless jobs and nights in flophouses continue to bear the fruit of fresh perspectives. The life is a teeming reservoir of material: anything—a traffic jam, a day at the track, a trip to the doctor's office—can be a source of inspiration. This will to excavate one's autobiography in the most straightforward and "unpoetic" style is the Bukowski legacy in all its mixed fallout over the last twenty-five years in American poetry: from lesser typists who think that copping an attitude and spilling their guts is all it takes, to original voices liberated to trust themselves in natural modes they might not have discovered without the master's barbaric example. That evident ease of expression, though, is earned. The short or long lines, the talky rhythms, the swiftness with which his utterances unfold, all the signature stylistic touches have been refined over thousands of hours at the typewriter— not in search of the single perfect phrase but in the repeated exercise of spontaneous composition.

Like some character out of Beckett, Bukowski's transparent persona in its despair, resignation and resolve-to-carry-on-in-spite-of-everything achieves a certain undeniable dignity. Boredom, illness, writer's block become occasions for writing. Even when the results are less than edifying—which is true about three-quarters of the time—there's something poignantly impressive in the struggle to give voice to what others might consider unspeakable or otherwise unworthy of poetry. Rather than discard the weaker poems, Bukowski includes them as part of the public record, the big picture of a work, a life, in progress. His lowbrow eloquence, such as it is, is an antidote to estheticism.

That's why you won't find Bukowski teaching, or being taught, in Master of Fine Arts programs. As he recounts in the new book, in a poem called "creative writing class":

> I noticed that the professor's advice
> on what to do
> and what not to do
> to become a writer was
> very pale and standard stuff
> that would lead to
> nowhere.

Not that even a singular path like his own leads anywhere, really: "the uselessness of the word is / evident," he writes in another poem.

> this incompleteness is all
> we have:
> we write the same things

over and over
again.
we are fools,
driven.

Such a bedrock existential admission, echoing the wisdom
of Ecclesiastes ("Vanity of vanities...all is vanity"), is as much
a self-critique as it is a philosophical truism. Preempting those
who would bother to take him seriously enough to criticize
his shortcomings, Bukowski is profoundly aware of his limitations as a writer. In his own primitively postmodern manner he
incorporates this self-awareness into an ongoing commentary
on the act of creation. His "narrative," especially in this latest
collection, deconstructs itself almost every step of the way.

At the same time he's utterly unapologetic for doing what
has kept him alive through an often hellish existence. At one
point, "after fifty years in the game," he kisses his typewriter
as a way of saying thank you. He is grateful for the occasional
fire lighting up his lines, for the mysterious friendliness of his
cats, for the taste of decent food after decades of chronic hunger, for the patience of his wife in putting up with him, for the
pleasure of feeling the night air on his balcony. Throughout
The Last Night of the Earth Poems—beyond or within the fear
of dying, the pathetic sense of the futility of it all, the sadness
of an aging body's failing and an imagination's waning—there
is a pervasive feeling of affirmation, of saying yes to life, even
as he rejects Sandburgian sentimentality.

the people survive to come up with flat fists full
of nothing.

I remember Carl Sandburg's poem, "The
People, Yes."
nice thought but completely inaccurate:
the people did not survive through a noble
strength but through lie, compromise and
guile.
I lived with these people, I am not so sure
what people Sandburg lived
with.
but his poem always pissed me off.
it was a poem that lied.
it is "The People, No."
then and now.
and it doesn't take a misanthrope to
say this.

Elsewhere he expands on this observation:

people are strange: they are constantly angered by
trivial things,
but on a major matter
like
totally wasting their lives,
they hardly seem to
notice…

Bukowski notices, and salvages what truth and comfort he
can by recording the trivial things.

Recording in his case means more than taking note of what
happens from day to day; it also means remembering everything: a feeling of contentment while eating in some greasy

spoon, a moment of peace in the library stacks as a miserable young man, the "clean gentle" satisfaction of a job unloading boxcars. It is striking how often the word *clean* appears in these poems, as if writing about the grimy past were an act of purification. It's also an act of recovery in every sense of the term. As time runs out on the life the mind works harder to resurrect what was, to savor the fading evidence, to find in what may have seemed meaningless at the time not a lesson or a moral but an essence of lived reality, and to fix it on the page in the plainest language. There is no illusion that the words are anything like the actual thing, the experience itself, but the written record can hint, can suggest, can solace, can inspire.

> I always resented all the years, the hours, the
> minutes I gave them as a working stiff, it
> actually hurt my head, my insides, it made me
> dizzy and a bit crazy—I couldn't understand the
> murdering of my years
> yet my fellow workers gave no signs of
> agony, many of them even seemed satisfied, and
> seeing them that way drove me almost as crazy as
> the dull and senseless work…
>
> I knew that I was dying.
> something in me said, go ahead, die, sleep, become as
> them, accept.
>
> then something else in me said, no, save the tiniest
> bit.
> it needn't be much, just a spark.
> a spark can set a whole forest on
> fire.

just a spark.
save it.

I think I did.
I'm glad I did.
what a lucky god damned
thing.

Bukowski's tendency toward solipsism is corrected by his regular attention to the world around him, both here-and-now and then-and-there. Though W. C. Williams is one precursor he seldom if ever invokes, Bukowski resembles him not only in his ear for ordinary speech but in the grounding of ideas in things. Language is not an end in itself, nor some opaque screen through which to question itself, but a tool for touching the facts of life, however unremarkable those facts may seem.

Does this mean that anybody can write a "Bukowski poem"? Well, yes and no. While he has spawned countless imitators, especially in the LA area, few of these mini-Bukowskis have anything like the naked desperation that gave rise to the original, and so no matter how well they may mimic the old man's mannerisms they can't approach the power of his expression. That's because the nonconformity of his early daring is what gave those defiant writings their sense of risk. Here was someone doing the poem his own way and fuck-you if you didn't like it. To model oneself on such an individual is to miss the point of his distinctive nerve, the lonely creation of a radically different voice. That there should now be an unofficial "school of Bukowski" may be a tribute to his funky genius but it makes no sense in light of his own accomplishment. The fact that the later Bukowski is a far gentler and in some ways more refined writer than he was at first does nothing to negate the integrity of his journey or to contradict its essential continuity. However many imitators he may have, he remains fundamentally inimitable.

What writers can learn from Bukowski, as from any author with heart enough to break out of the safety of convention, is to listen for one's own deepest, most authentic music, no matter how discordant it may sound, and let it rip. The bottles of booze, the filthy ashtrays, the puke-stained undershirts, the scummy one-nighters and other unsavory images so often associated with the Bukowski legend—even the seemingly ragged yet sneakily crafty style of his verse—are of little consequence beside the relentless determination he has demonstrated to carry on regardless of the revulsion or adulation his work evokes. Indeed, he seems to have as much contempt for his admirers as for his critics—maybe more. At least the critics offer a stimulating opposition analogous to the challenges the rest of his life has provided: he thrives on resistance. The fawners, the fellow outlaw-geniuses, the ass-kissers asking for favors are, to judge from his documentation of their behavior, a pain in the ass. Though Bukowski has in fact been known to be kind to his fans, from a distance at least—answering their letters, responding to solicitations from unknown editors of upstart magazines—his aloofness from the literary fray, proceeding with his project at whatever cost, is exemplary.

Like an aging boxer losing his speed or a tired slugger whose "batting average has dropped to / .231" (recurrent tropes in the *Last Night* poems for his fate as an ancient veteran), Bukowski sees retirement coming inexorably in the only way that can take him out of the game. Death, a favorite theme for many years, is ever present in this book, a punch line for the ultimate joke at his own expense. We see the poet stoically enduring tuberculosis, cancer, all the indignities of decrepitude, yet somehow resisting destruction by writing it all down in meticulous detail. His tone is less pugnacious than elegiac as he tries out variations on the dirge that will finally honor his own demise. Given the unlikelihood of his having lived this long, for all we know he may go on to crank out a thousand more pages of reportage, adding a few last-ditch volumes to his already awesome output before the cosmic powers call his number. Either way, even a selective reading of his forty-five books to date reveals a human being of extraordinary character, an indomitable personality who has grown in stature with every document he produces. Whether any individual piece has the requisite artistry or grace or truth to hold up over time remains to be seen—for my money there are many. But odds are that in terms of a life's work there are few contemporaries who can claim to have made a more substantial, accessible, entertaining and enduring contribution.

1992

3 *"The Words Have Saved My Ass"*

After my review of Charles Bukowski's *The Last Night of the Earth Poems* appeared last year in *Poetry Flash* I sent the author a copy of the published piece. It was the latest of some half dozen essays I'd done on his work over the years—my personal effort to give him the serious critical attention I felt he deserved—and I enclosed a note half-jokingly informing him that this was the last thing I was going to write about him until his eightieth birthday. True to his record as a reliable correspondent, he replied promptly with a letter that began: "So, you're not going to write any more about me until I'm 80? You sure you can last that long?"

I'm still not sure what's harder to believe, his death last month at seventy-three or the fact that he lasted that long. Hospitalized with a bleeding ulcer at thirty-five and informed by his doctors that alcohol was killing him, Bukowski upon release immediately resumed drinking and—having failed up to that point as a fiction writer—began writing poetry in earnest. This combination of antisocial activities kept him going for nearly another forty years. The work he produced in that time, the poems and stories and novels, sustained a consistently high level of quality even as his style evolved from one informed by rage and pain and fear to a gentler, more philosophical acceptance of life's inevitable griefs. The fact that he'd endured so much and continued to write so well made him seem indestructible. And that's why it's so hard to believe he's dead.

It's not as if he was a youthful talent unexpectedly taken away in his prime, much less a venerable icon whose development the literati had witnessed eternally from early promise through ripening brilliance into a softly drooping yet immortal dotage. No, Bukowski was born old. By the time he emerged as a notable writer in the mid-1960s he was already well past forty and seemed somehow ancient with the cumulative suffering of a terrible childhood and tormented adolescence followed by the miserable existence of a hopelessly alcoholic adult. Poverty-stricken, violence-prone, bouncing from job to job, he wasn't exactly a poster boy for the noble hardworking proletariat; by all accounts, especially his own, he was quite the unsavory character. His poems in the little magazines, his stories and columns in the underground press were barbaric eruptions out of the literary cityscape, exceeding in their sub-poetic intensity even the rebellious excesses of the Beats. To this day, despite his obvious importance, most self-respecting critics won't touch his work with a ten-foot pole.

While his books may never have made the bestseller lists, according to publisher John Martin of Black Sparrow Press Bukowski is the largest-selling contemporary American poet. Martin ought to know. It is mainly through the sales of Bukows-ki's prolific output that Black Sparrow has grown to become one of the most distinguished and successful literary publish-ers on the planet. This hasn't kept the critics from ignoring him. As he wrote to me in 1987, responding to a review I'd done of his collection *You Get So Alone at Times That It Just Makes Sense*: "If I were a bitchy poet, and maybe I am, I would say, fine, that there is a review, bad or good. What I have found is that no matter any number of books that I have written, there are seldom reviews of any of them.

"So, whatever the reason, you've broken through into some-where."

The critical attention he has received tends to range from a kind of awestruck adulation in the little magazines to an amusedly superior and dismissive acknowledgment in big-cir-culation highbrow periodicals that this wild man does have a certain exotic appeal but he's really just a kooky LA underbelly cult figure. The fact that there was so little sensible commen-tary between these extremes is what moved me back in the mid-1970s to start reviewing his books and has kept me at it ever since. Reclusive and maybe a little misanthropic, Bukowski, in a letter of 1984, on receiving the clip of my review of his collection *War All the Time*, seemed somewhat relieved to have stayed out of the mainstream: "Overseas fame while having limited fame here is the best, the gods are looking after me: I can walk through a dozen supermarkets, or up and down the main drags of major cities (American) and nobody will bother me. This allows me to live a normal life which only I can despoil. Most indents upon me are made through the mail. An occasional rare and real letter deserves an answer."

Why is Bukowski so widely and avidly read? I think it's because his writing, both fiction and poetry, is so honest, personal, straightforward, funny and easy to understand. He's appreciated by people who don't read a lot of other poetry because they don't have the patience to decipher its obfuscations nor the desire to worship it as Art. They're looking, I suppose, for stories and poems that might relate usefully to their lives. Which is not to say Bukowski lacks admirers among the intelligentsia; avant-garde readers and poets noticed his uniqueness early on, and he continues to be one of the most emulated voices in verse. As distinctively as Walt Whitman or William Carlos Williams—or, in other ways, Henry Miller—Bukowski opened American language to a radical vernacular no one had heard before. The raw authenticity of his naked persona, the vulgar simplicity of his style, the sincerity of his anguish, the depth of his salty humor, the out-of-the-ballpark wildness of his desperate imagination resounded in the souls of countless younger writers (especially here on the West Coast) in search of a poetics equal to their experience. Bukowski proved that to be a poet, or a reader of poetry, you didn't need to be highly schooled or refined. All the better if you were driven to some troubled below-good-and-evil eloquence by the real feeling and spontaneous expression of unspeakably ordinary events.

I remember the astonishment and delight of discovering, after reading his poems in the littles, his 1969 book from Black Sparrow *The Days Run Away Like Wild Horses Over the Hills*. The poems were alive with the flames of raving talk and the unpredictable vision of the greatest nightmares. They were entertaining yet profoundly grave in their daring encounter with everyday tragedy. As new books followed regularly over the next twenty-five years—issued by Black Sparrow in beautifully designed editions—I was continually amazed and inspired by the author's ability to lift the baseness of his daily life, past and present, actual and imaginary, into a high and at the same time down-to-earth art.

In early 1985, when he was already a superstar of the international underground, I wrote requesting an interview. He answered: "Got your letter. Yes, I know you are an Ace. And can handle such matters as interviews much better than almost anybody. But I've got to say 'no' because I'm just burned-out over such things. Went through an experience—twice—of talking my ass off for hours to people who were going to do a biography on me. Nothing happened. Not that that is important, it's just the energy of hours wasted. Then did a film bit with some Italians and one other guy and they all got to squabbling, stealing from one another, threatening lawsuits, all that…the cans just sit there full of hours of my babble…Finally did another film bit for another group and it worked, was shown full blast…Then talked FOR SIXTY HOURS for a video. I believe it began showing on National TV in France, prime time, this January 7 or 8. It is supposed to run in segments of from three to six minutes for a great many nights, depending on how long it takes somebody to bomb the station.

"What I'm trying to say here is THAT I'M SICK OF TALKING ABOUT MYSELF…

"The main thing about writing is to write, not to talk about writing."

Bukowski wrote, all right, and appeared never to break stride in the process. He made it look easy. For him it *was* easy: he just opened his veins and the stories came pouring out. The ever-increasing clarity of his style was earned through long hours and years of patient composition. With booze as his muse, with classical music on the radio, with various inscrutable yet sympathetic cats as companions, with a succession of faithful typewriters and eventually in the last years a computer, he let flow anything that occurred to him, from mundane happenings of the moment to recollections of his abused youth, from chronicles of deadly jobs and tales of dingy bars to unsparing accounts of poisonous love affairs, all reported with the vivid eye of the participant-observer and flashes of painful but unflinching insight. His work is easy to read, unambiguous, disarmingly open; more than once I've been drawn through a whole book in one long night. Bukowski's rough music is oddly consoling: you figure if this guy can outlive his difficulties, anybody can.

"In the factories, in the post office, in all the lousy jobs, I was always known as the kind of white-trash good guy with just something a little bit wrong with him. So, the fights with the big blacks in the alley at break-time only showed them a kind of dim kindly clown, albeit with a seemingly useless courage.

"I took that from the factories of day to the bars of night, going into the alleys with the largest beasts I could find, and often not doing too badly.

"But I was never on the macho-kick. I was somehow trying to force my way through doors that would not open. And I tried that with women too. Don't get me wrong. I only wanted some sound, some sense, some minor luck.

"But all the men I fought, all the women I fucked, there was some lacking of connection, somewhere. Somewhere."

That 1987 letter goes on: "What I am trying to say—the magic was always missing. And getting to read the poets, to me, everything seemed to be missing. They were just fucking off, playing tricks, they were ultimately comfortable…

"I thought I might try something else: simply say what was. It got me hatred and expulsion but I still think I got it down fair. But you know, maybe not literary. I starved my ass for a week or two or a ten year or two to work that out. I hated the poets living and dead, the best of the centuries and those accepted and revered at the moment, I didn't really hate them, I just couldn't read them…

"Well, I came in to fight and I am still at it…Nearing seventy, I still don't like the scene…I still think the words should rip across the page in immaculate fire."

By the time he wrote these pugnacious lines he was physically pretty comfortable himself, living quietly with his wife in San Pedro, driving his black BMW, using his American Express Gold Card, spending his days at the racetrack and his nights at the desk with expensive wine. In the published poetry and prose much of his earlier angst had given way to a humble gratitude for his good fortune as he continued fearlessly to record his simultaneous rise and decline into old age. Not that success ever turned him soft. Tender and even sentimental at times, undeniably much mellower than in the down days in Los Angeles, the aged poet remained to the end lucid, witty, tough like the veteran street-fighter he was. His prose grew increasingly clean and streamlined, the best of his lyric poems conversational but concise, pared to the essence of the author's thought. Most moving of all for me were the narrative poems: with a few precise strokes, short lines racing down the page, Bukowski could tell the most evocatively detailed and poignant stories. What he lacked in range he more than made up for in depth. Acutely conscious of his limitations, he was also sure of his powers.

"For me, the words seem to bite into the paper better than ever," he wrote in last year's letter. "A writer should get better as he gets older: there's more to work with, a larger canvas. But most writers get lucky too early, then get the fat head, get greedy, get dull, fall apart. They are short distance runners. Too bad. That's why we have so much crappy literature about, the slim volumes, the slight pages of Selected Works. It's disheartening: everything wilts away."

Everything but Bukowski. His books have kept getting bigger, and if the percentage of extra-base hits has dropped a bit over the years it hardly matters. His accomplishment is cumulative, expansive, uneven, one of the more exhaustive and candid accounts of any life on record, its thousands of pages testifying to the author's conviction that life is finally more important than art—and yet without the voluminous art the life might not have been possible. Bukowski kept writing right to the end as if, or because, his life depended on it. Black Sparrow editor/publisher Martin was always there to catch the overflow and sort it out into books. As Bukowski wrote me in 1984 and I confirmed last year on a visit to Black Sparrow in Santa Rosa, Martin "has quite a buildup of unpublished material from a couple of decades. There's a very good chance, if the world is still here, that he can publish a new Bukowski book each year for a good five or six or seven years, maybe longer depending upon how long I continue to drink this good wine. Of course, that will all be beyond me: I'll be down in Hades playing the Horses."

Martin recently edited *Run with the Hunted: A Charles Bukowski Reader*, a biographically organized selection from his works, for HarperCollins. Between that 400-page tome, the books in print and the ones to come, you can bet that recognition of his prodigious achievement will only grow now that he's gone. Even the English departments may yet acknowledge his existence.

Up until now, sad to say, Bukowski is probably best known in the US as the writer of the dreadful 1987 movie *Barfly*. This minor work, equal to some of his weaker short stories, was the old man's breakthrough into the pop-culture mainstream. Even then, bopping with the celebrities for a minute, he retained his identity as an outsider and resisted the meatgrinder of Hollywood hero-worship. Bukowski stayed out of his reputation's way with a resolve rarely matched by any such celebrated writer. He admired Robinson Jeffers, another California recluse whose anti-humanist philosophy was even more misanthropic than his own. (Jeffers too had come through LA before retreating to his Carmel cliff.) Rejected by New York's literary-industrial complex, Bukowski pressed on unstoppably with his project, contributing to obscure small magazines at the request of their prestigeless but dedicated editors—the same kinds of editors who first brought his work to print—and establishing himself as a rock-solid alternative to the tastemakers.

"With me," he said in that letter a year ago, "the whole matter has been a day by day, night by night journey. The words were put down, the drinks were drunk, and there still seems more to do. What I mean is, stopping now would be hell. The words have saved my ass, it's as simple as that. There's always something more to overcome, to live through. Death's coming, that's all right but it's not here yet. The BMW is now an Acura and there's a swimming pool and a Jacuzzi. It's in my writing." These are not the words of a conspicuous consumer but of a man who has survived a lifetime of ordeals to enjoy the ridiculous luxuries of his luck.

From the brutalized boyhood recorded so compassionately in the 1982 novel *Ham on Rye* ("a book I could only write from many years distance") through the low-rent squalor of his middle years and the first glimpses of literary success—gruelingly recounted in his other great novel, *Women* (1978)—to the wisdom and equanimity of his prosperous sixties and seventies, Bukowski's integrity is unbroken. His work is a beacon for those who would honestly face the wounded beauty of their lives and turn it into a battle-scarred art. Like the poet's punched-out, alcohol-ravaged, acne-pitted yet strangely handsome face, even the imperfections of such an effort can be heroic, full of unkillable character and an enduring legacy of courage.

1994

In These States

An Unsung Master:
The Many Lives of
James Laughlin

The genesis of James Laughlin's New Directions Publishing Corporation is legendary. Laughlin, not yet twenty, a Harvard freshman and aspiring poet bored and restless in that academic setting, fled to Europe, first to spend part of the summer working for Gertrude Stein in France, and then in search of instruction at Ezra Pound's "Ezuversity" in Rapallo, Italy. At the time, in 1934, despite his noxious anti-Semitism and his increasingly eccentric politics, Pound was the cranky Godfather of American literary Modernism, preaching the Make It New! gospel, issuing polemical pronunciamentos, and promoting his chosen writers, ancient and contemporary. Stein of course considered herself the Mother of all Modernists and, as Laughlin recalled later, "Gertrude and Ezra didn't quite get on"—Stein dismissing Pound as "a village explainer" and Pound referring to Stein as "that old tub of guts." Undaunted by such powerful and contentious personalities, Laughlin (pronounced Locklin) stayed and studied with Pound in Rapallo for six months before the master, with characteristic tact, declared his poems "worthless" and told him to "do something useful."

Back at Harvard two years later, with the financial support of his family's Pittsburgh steel fortune, Laughlin launched the first of his New Directions anthologies, a proving ground for the work of such then-disreputable writers as Pound, Stein, William Carlos Williams, E. E. Cummings, Marianne Moore, Henry Miller, Jean Cocteau, Kenneth Rexroth, William Saroyan, Delmore Schwartz and many others.

Eventually, in 1939, at Pound's insistence (because "then your father will give you some money"), Laughlin completed his bachelor's degree at Harvard. By then he had already become a champion of the avant-garde, beginning a long career of publishing books by an all-star lineup of American and international authors, many of whom remain consistent sellers on the New Directions backlist. The press operated in the red for more than twenty years, but Laughlin was confident that his kinds of writers were a long-term investment whose works would sooner or later find their readers. In his Preface to the 1937 New Directions annual the upstart editor makes clear his mission: "The only useful function which a book like New Directions can fulfill is to get into print good writing which otherwise would go unpublished…"

He goes on to pick a fight with the powers that be: "Anyone can see that there is a chip on my shoulder. I am angry with the big publishers because they are not doing their jobs… In spite of the money which they must be making on their wretched bestsellers they are not doing what they should for the pure writer.

"Who is the pure writer? Simply, he is the writer who writes for God and not the Devil…"

Framing his argument for experimental writing and publishing as nothing less than a battle of good against evil, Laughlin went on for the next six decades to establish himself as arguably the preeminent literary publisher of his time in English, resisting the temptations of the commercial mainstream that had altered the course (and paid the bills) of other serious bookmen. For the next two or three generations he ran his own kind of university for readers who had what he called "linguistic curiosity," an interest in new kinds of creative language. Laughlin and New Directions were and are a model of editorial independence and artistic integrity for what was to become, from the 1960s onward, an explosion of small presses and little magazines. By that time New Directions Paperbooks, with their distinctive black-and-white covers, were magical objects in the hands of any self-respecting bohemian intellectual, and the diverse poets and fiction writers whose work appeared under the ND imprint—Dylan Thomas, Octavio Paz, Paul Bowles, Pablo Neruda, Lawrence Ferlinghetti, Robert Duncan, García Lorca, Nabokov, Kafka, Denise Levertov, Gary Snyder, Celine, Borges, Valéry, Rilke and the irrepressible Rexroth, to name a few—were all to leave a lasting mark on literature.

Laughlin's family fortune, which was not to become his own until he was well into his publishing career, is insufficient to explain his persistence in promoting the kinds of books he knew could not compete commercially. He had not only vision but ambition—and the courage to put his money where his mouth was.

The first New Directions book to sell more than a million copies was to come, improbably, by way of Henry Miller, who had read Herman Hesse's *Siddhartha* in Europe and informed Laughlin that this novel could be a hit in the United States.

Miller's own writing was so anti-commercial when it wasn't downright scandalous (Laughlin declined to publish *Tropic of Cancer* and *Tropic of Capricorn* for fear, he explained to Miller, of offending his Aunt Leila and thereby cutting off a source of funding; he begged off on Nabokov's *Lolita* for the same reason) that he was the last person you'd expect to care about sales. But Miller, like many of Laughlin's other authors, was an active co-conspirator in keeping the enterprise alive, part of a network of contributing editors who offered critiques, complaints and recommendations, providing the publisher with a steady stream of advice and talent-scouting.

No one, after Pound's initial coaching, was more influential in this regard than Rexroth, who constantly harangued from the West Coast, encouraging Laughlin to sign up certain writers, berating him for publishing others and generally being the know-it-all Buddhist-anarcho-pacifist California counterpoint to Pound. That Laughlin remained professionally functional and socially friendly with these and so many other extreme personages, some of whom hated each other, and continued to work effectively with all, is testimony to his psychosocial, diplomatic and entrepreneurial skills. From persuading Dr. Williams that switching to a bigger publisher where he might make more money would be a disaster for both Williams and New Directions, to sending Dylan Thomas an occasional twenty dollars in response to his begging letters, to rescuing Tennessee Williams from some female admirer who wouldn't leave him alone, Laughlin was a master of interpersonal relations. Most of these relationships are documented in his voluminous correspondence—six volumes of which (exchanges with W. C. Williams, Pound, Rexroth, Miller, Schwartz and Thomas Merton) have thus far been published by Norton. He saved and filed every-thing, including carbons of his own letters, and bequeathed to Harvard on his death in 1997 his entire archive of 1,298 boxes of material, with the stipulation that everything be catalogued within two years—otherwise it would go to Yale. The shrewd-ness and foresight of the old man's strategy for keeping his papers available to scholars rather than stashed away in some inaccessible vault is typical of the way he ran his business.

Current New Directions publisher Griselda Ohannessian, who has been with the company for nearly fifty years, remem-bers her former boss as a rather complex individual. "There were so many aspects of his character," she told me. "He changed a lot over the years. He was—not arrogant exactly, but a bit precious and cocky" when he was younger, later becoming "more thoughtful and understanding" toward other people. An emblematic image she has of Laughlin, a lifelong Pittsburgh Pirates fan, is of him sitting at his desk on a summer day, smok-ing a cigar while reviewing manuscripts and attending to other business, the radio in his office tuned to the Pirates game.

Harvard met the cataloguing deadline, and this past winter celebrated its accomplishment and Laughlin's contribution with an exhibition of letters, manuscripts, proofs, artwork, photos and other memorabilia from the Laughlin/ND col-lection now at Houghton Library. The Lamont Library next door hosted a standing-room-only symposium where Laugh-lin biographer Ian MacNiven (who estimates his book will be ready in three years), fellow poet and publisher Jonathan Williams, and essayist and translator Eliot Weinberger shared their ideas, anecdotes, insights and speculations about the meaning of what "JL," or "J" had managed to do. It was clear from the conversation that we're just beginning to comprehend what a towering figure he was, over and above his six-foot-five physique.

As Weinberger pointed out, Laughlin "had the self-deprecation of the exceedingly tall." He not only pretended to have become a publisher due to his failure as a would-be poet, but he kept his practice and increasing skill and depth as a writer of verse pretty much out of sight until the last years of his life, revealing finally what Weinberger called "one of the secret treasures of American poetry."

Ferlinghetti's City Lights Books brought out Laughlin's *Selected Poems 1935–1985* in 1986 without much fanfare. Most readers of poetry in the United States still considered Laughlin mainly a publisher; he had published Ferlinghetti among other writers of the San Francisco Renaissance and Beat movements, and now it appeared that Ferlinghetti was merely returning the favor. Anyone who took a close look at that book might have realized that the founder of New Directions was a real poet, not some over-privileged self-indulgent dilettante; but it was only in the 1990s that the full force and weight of his poetry started to make itself felt—though, again, hardly anyone noticed. In 1989 Copper Canyon Press brought out a lovely collection called *The Bird of Endless Time,* whose title poem is typical of Laughlin's delicate lyric clarity:

> Your fingers touch me like a bird's wing
> like the feathers of the bird that returns
>
> every hundred years to brush against a
> peak in the Himalayas and not until the
>
> rock's been worn away will time and the

kalpas end   why do I think of the fable

when I'm close with you   surely because
I want so many lives to feel your touch.

Aside from the casual reference to the Hindu kalpas, or eons
of creation, a nod to the poet's ecumenical studies in world
culture, these lines also illustrate Laughlin's signature typo-
graphic metric, which he said he had learned from Williams:
visually measured couplets in which the second line is no more
than two typewriter spaces longer or shorter than the line that
precedes it. "It's a very soulful metric," he told Weinberger in
an interview. And it gives his voice on the page a bit of its classical atmosphere.

With *The Collected Poems of James Laughlin* publisher
Moyer Bell, in 1994, made a five-hundred-and-fifty-page case
for this author as a major American poet. To discover such a
volume in a secondhand bookstore, as I did just a couple of
years ago, is to experience the kind of revelation bookshop
prowlers live for. The poems spoke with a candor and wit and
subtle simplicity and exquisite syncopation I could scarcely
recall encountering anywhere else, except perhaps in Dudley
Fitts's translations from the Greek Anthology, which, as it happens, New Directions had published early on. (Fitts had been
Laughlin's English teacher at prep school.) Here's a little statement on poetics that speaks to some of the virtues of Laughlin's verse:

Some People Think

that poetry should be a-
dorned or complicated I'm

　　　　not so sure I think I'll
　　　　take the simple statement

　　　　in plain speech compress-
　　　　ed to brevity I think that

　　　　will do all I want to do.

Not that he's always this succinct, but even in the poems that go on for a page or two he seems to be following Pound's advice to "make it simple" and Williams's advice to "make what / you saw as plain as you can" and Rexroth's advice to "boil it down but boil / it with a cold flame."

As if *The Collected Poems* weren't enough, New Directions followed, in Laughlin's final years, with new collections: *The Man in the Wall, The Secret Room,* and *Poems New and Selected,* a phenomenal flowering of creative work for a writer in his seventies and eighties. What's striking about Laughlin's last poems—and there are a lot of them—is that the poet, having mostly retired as an active publisher in New York City and spending more time at home in rural Connecticut, seems to have fully come into his own now that, instead of running a business, he was free to write with minimal distraction. He ransacks memory, and dreams, and everyday life, and his vast reading, as if savoring ever more appreciatively the experiences and people and emotions and sensations he knows won't come again. He speaks directly to this theme in a brief poem called "The Consolations":

　　　　The treasures of old age
　　　　Are the little adventures
　　　　　　of the imagination.

A beautiful face recalls
    another
That was so much loved
    long ago
And we console ourselves
Saying "I'm young again."

But all is not wistful nostalgia; the bite of the satirist is also sharp, as in "Poets on Stilts":

Writing on stilts is in vogue
these days. The taller the stilts
the easier to be in fashion.
Very few poets now want to walk
with their feet on the ground,
they might get their shoes wet.

                ...Altitude
makes the poet feel important
and it gets him into the club.

But a word of warning to
stiltwalkers. The higher they
fall from their stilts, the
bigger the smash when they
hit the pavement.

And most of all the poet of love, in all his passion and folly and knowledge and crafty sentiment, declines to retire; here he writes, in "Elusive Time":

In love it may be dangerous
to reckon on time to count

on it   time's here and then
it's gone   I'm not thinking

of death or disaster but of
the slippage the unpredictable

disappearance of days on which
we were depending for happiness.

Unlike some other modernist masters, Laughlin is a poet
one reads for pleasure, not from a sense of duty or as an intellectual exercise. While his reading of the early Greek and
Roman poets is evident throughout, and his erudition finds
its expression in numerous allusions and direct references or
quotations, and he occasionally breaks into French or German or Latin or Greek or Italian for a few lines or an entire
poem (for which he kindly provides an English translation),
there's nothing lofty or pretentious about his style. The humor
and humility and genial earnestness are completely engaging.
He can write of personal tragedy—of having to identify Dylan
Thomas's corpse at a New York morgue, or of cleaning up
the blood from his son's suicide—in such an understated,
matter-of-fact way that it's all the more devastating. And the
invocations of women, of wives and lovers and near misses,
are as tender and poignant and sexy as any such poems I've
ever read.

A TRANSLATION

How did you decide to translate me
from one language to another   let's

say from the English of friendship

to the French of lovers   we'd known

each other half a year when one day
as we were talking (it was about one

of your drawings) suddenly you curl-
ed yourself against me and drew my

lips down to yours   it was so deft
an alternance from one language to

the other as if to say yes you can
speak French to me now if you wish.

These are poems of an examined life, philosophical, yet also
with the sportsman's appreciation of the sensory rush for its
own sake—Laughlin was a mountaineer and an accomplished
downhill skier who pioneered that sport in the United States
by opening a lodge in Utah, another of the entrepreneurial
escapades pulled off when he wasn't busy being a publisher.

Beyond the sheer pleasure they afford, Laughlin's verses
are a tonic antidote to rhetorical excess and metaphysical
mumbo jumbo. Writers can learn a lot from his example about
the power of economy and the strength of poetic technique
so deft and light in its touch as to give the illusion of effort-
lessness. He follows Wordsworth's still-useful admonition
that poetry should speak directly to the common reader, not
in some mannered code encrypted for initiates. In a curious
and unlikely way, which he would no doubt dispute, Laughlin resembles Charles Bukowski, a poet whose work he found
"vulgar and corny" and alien to his own more elitist tastes.
But like Bukowski, Laughlin speaks of ordinary experience in

a disarmingly intimate style, almost unliterary in its simplicity. And while Bukowski cultivated the hardboiled persona of the drunken racetrack bum and good-for-nothing bard of the sub-working class, in contrast to Laughlin's casual dignity of the cosmobohemian aristocrat, both vividly embody Whitman's notion that whoever touches his book touches a man.

Why did Laughlin wait so long to reveal himself as a poet? Did he feel so overshadowed by the greats he was publishing that it dimmed his confidence in the value of his own creative work? Or was his confidence in himself so solid that he felt the poems could wait to be published because their quality guaranteed they would outlast their author? As Jonathan Williams noted at the Harvard symposium, the Latin poets from whom Laughlin had learned so much—Catullus, Horace, Martial—"don't look quite as good as they used to, compared to Laughlin." Maybe it was the survival of these ancient models, the freshness of their voices, even in translation, that convinced Laughlin his own efforts had plenty of time to find their readers.

As one of those belated readers, I've been lucky to come across his books at bargain prices on remainder tables in some of my favorite bookshops, but it's sad that they've already dropped off the retail shelves. Surely New Directions will keep his books in print, at least in paperback, just as Laughlin did for his own writers, in the likelihood that as years go by the interest in his poems will increase. His press, in its own ongoing, low-key way, continues to thrive as an outlet for current innovators (W. G. Sebald, Mary Karr, Bei Dao, Michael Palmer) as well as for modern classics from around the world. And in a poetically just example of the prophet's vision being vindicated by acceptance into the bosom of the institution where he began as a radical misfit, Harvard has picked up the historic mission of keeping Laughlin's paper trail intact.

For anyone of less than scholarly curiosity, the poems alone are an eloquent record of an exceptionally well-lived life.

2001

Denise Levertov,
Rival of Nightingales

Amid the ambient cacophony of end-of-the-millennium American culture, the death of Denise Levertov last December 20 scarcely registered in the popular consciousness; but to those of us for whom she was, at one time or another, a guiding light of lyric integrity, the news was heartbreaking. Levertov's mastery of open form, the musical beauty and sensory clarity of her language, the nakedness of her self-revelation without ever seeming "self-indulgent," her vigorous spirituality and soulful politics, her prolific and practically nonstop poetic production for nearly sixty years and her generosity toward younger writers combine to make her one of the essential poets of our time.

Levertov herself started out quite young, sending some of her poems to T. S. Eliot (and receiving a lengthy reply) at the age of twelve. At seventeen her first published poem appeared in her native England, and by the time she moved to the States in her mid-twenties she had already been discovered by the astute editorial eye of Kenneth Rexroth. She soon became associated with the Black Mountain school—Charles Olson, Robert Duncan, Robert Creeley, et al.—and with an added boost from a couple of other San Francisco–based poet-editors, Weldon Kees and Lawrence Ferlinghetti, she eventually found her way to James Laughlin's indispensable New Directions, which has remained her publisher ever since.

In a string of astonishing books brought out by New Directions from the late 1950s to the early 1970s (reissued now in three collected volumes), a time of extraordinary richness in US poetry, Levertov emerged as a singular star, again and again delivering poems of startling beauty and simplicity, deploying a deeply sophisticated technical skill with unmatched subtlety, grace and emotional honesty. I can name few other poets—most notably Robert Duncan—who are Levertov's peers in effective use of the page as a visual/vocal field of poetic notation. Without ever being flashy in her virtuosity, she seemed to have an uncanny sense of where and when to break or indent a line or to open space between phrases, to give the poem a visual rhythm that fit precisely not only its sound but its tone, its feeling and its meaning.

Deriving this style from her own intuitive synthesis of the prosodic advances of Pound, Williams, and Charles Olson's theory of "Protective Verse," Levertov modestly referred to her technique as one of "organic form," an open approach to composition every bit as rigorous as the strictest traditional verse, requiring the most sensitive attunement to the flow of language and image, thought and feeling, sound and silence, type and space on the page. Far from being an end in itself, this dazzling facility with form enabled her to respond artistically to her experience and surroundings in ways that felt to the reader not only necessary but inevitable. Whether writing about the streets and subways of New York City, the intimacies and complexities of love, or some subtle detail of the natural land-scape—a leaf, a shade of light, a scent in the air—she responded with an instinctive fidelity that appeared virtually artless.

Later, of course, from the Vietnam War on, Levertov became a political poet, a voice of protest and resistance, even as she continued her explorations in the realms of nature, spirit and personal sentiment. For me, the most effective of her overtly political poems derive their power from the same inwardness and intimacy that illumine the earlier work: that sense of faithful observation, attention to detail and measured musical speech. Her moral vision and lyric gifts, applied to the horrors of war in books like *The Sorrow Dance* and *Relearning the Alphabet*, convey the grief and outrage born of US military atrocities more eloquently than some of her later, more explicit rhetorical denunciations. Yet whether observing "In dust / the lace designs incised / by feet of beetles" or, more appallingly, "another child with its feet blown off," the sensibility we meet in Levertov's poems is integrated, open to whatever it encounters and poised to respond with its transformative instrument, song.

It is testimony to her breadth of soul that, for all her opposi-tional politics—her antiwar, antinuclear and pro-environmental work—Levertov never became an ideologue. She continued to cite among her models the famously conservative and estheti-cally "elitist" poets Rilke and Stevens, both of whom fed her hunger for transcendence. For Levertov, mobilization of her esthetic imagination in service to a spiritual vision was no less vital a moral imperative than the need to march on picket lines or speak at rallies. Her humility in the face of life's awesome mysteries precluded her assuming a posture of self-righteous-ness, moral superiority, ironic detachment or intellectual arrogance. Her poems are neither trendy nor "cutting edge," but they're consistently engaged—in sharp perception, passionate feeling, intense desire for decency and justice, and deep appreciation of beauty.

Though I couldn't have explained it this way at the time, it was my admiration for all these qualities that inspired me, while suffering through graduate school, to send her a note of gratitude. She responded by asking if I was the same "Steve Kessler" who had recently made the news by burning his draft card at some demonstration. (I was not, but if I had been, it would have impressed her far more than anything I was writing.) A few years later, in 1972, at the age of twenty-five, I summoned the courage to send her a few of my poems. Again she wrote back more quickly than I expected: "I feel reality in your poems, nothing phony"—which was about as much encouragement as I could have hoped for.

Sometime after that—it must have been 1974 or 1975—she wrote to me, requesting I send some work. She was editing a special section of *The American Poetry Review* devoted to little-known poets, and was also serving as poetry editor of a new political magazine, unnamed as yet but soon to be known as *Mother Jones*. She received what I sent her with gratifying enthusiasm, and that's how it happened that in the spring of 76, when I was on the East Coast en route to Spain and she was teaching at Tufts and living in Somerville, I got to be her houseguest for a couple of days, meeting her in person for the first time and incidentally witnessing some of her work habits.

Two things especially struck me. One was that, in her three-story house, she had set up three different offices—one for her own poetry, one for personal business and correspondence, and the third for her work as an editor (before her stint with *Mother Jones* she had for years been poetry editor of *The Nation*). Denise Levertov, I realized, was not just a poet, she was a poetry industry, with her labors efficiently divided even though her writing life was somehow a seamless whole. When I asked her how she managed not to be exhausted by her various commitments—writing, politics, editing, teaching—she replied that one thing fed the other, so that rather than deplete her creative energies, her multiple activities invigorated them.

The other telling detail of her working life was revealed in the typescript of a poem she showed me: she triple-spaced the lines of her verse, as if to give each word more room to breathe, more emphasis, more resonance as an individual unit of composition. This may seem like an unremarkable observation, but it has stayed with me as a simple graphic example, a reminder to make every syllable count.

In the course of a move some years ago a box of books I had shipped from California to New York broke open somewhere in between and most of the contents were lost. As fate would have it, they were all my favorite poetry books, including several by Levertov, which I've never seen again. Since then, in my habitual prowlings through secondhand bookstores, I've often searched for copies of such vintage Levertov titles as *With Eyes at the Back of Our Heads, The Jacob's Ladder,* and *O Taste and See,* superb collections of her lyric brilliance in the bloom of its first great flowering. But apparently, once they own them, people don't recycle these books; the poems are kept as permanent resources, reservoirs of inspiration.

In *Breathing the Water* (1987—there are two new collec-

tions since then, *Evening Train* and *Sands of the Well*, her latest) there is a little poem which, while hardly representing the
breadth and depth of its author's achievement, might serve for
the moment as a fitting epitaph for a poet whose disappearance—mostly unnoticed by the multitudes—has subtly impov-
erished the world, just as her presence subtly enriched it. The
poem is called "The Mockingbird of Mockingbirds." Denise
Levertov writes:

> A greyish bird
> the size perhaps of two plump sparrows,
> fallen in some field,
> soon flattened, a dry
> mess of feathers—
> and no one knows
> this was a prince among his kind,
> virtuoso of virtuosos,
> lord of a thousand songs,
> debonair, elaborate in invention, fantasist,
> rival of nightingales.

1998

Robert Bly Unbound

1 Shaman in San José

Under the subtly enervating drone and glare of fluorescent lights, poet Robert Bly gave his annual San José reading last Thursday night to an adoring audience in the SJSU Student Union. Bly, still feisty but growing more venerable every year, played his dulcimer, told jokes and fairytales, used various masks for dramatic effect, recited translations from Rilke and Rumi, expounded on the unconscious, read new and old poems of his own with his famous gesticulations, and accidentally sat on his glasses.

It's been fascinating, sometimes annoying and often inspiring to observe Bly's evolution over the years, When I first met him, in 1967, he had already been active for more than a decade—mainly by way of his magazine, *The Fifties* (later *The Sixties*)—as an agent of change and growth in American poetry. His poems, translations, essays, parodies and polemics on contemporary writing made healthy waves in the literary complacency of the period. Along with the Beats and the Black Mountain poets (Charles Olson, Robert Creeley and their followers), Bly helped resurrect the vital energy withering under the weight of an exhausted English tradition.

I recall that 1967 reading in upstate New York as a good one—the poet's images resonating in my student mind deep into the night—but Bly was fairly conventional in his presentation. Conservatively dressed, standing behind the lectern, he didn't make a particularly *dramatic* impression.

In the course of the next few years—through the depths of the Vietnam War—Bly's act changed radically and so did his reputation. Wearing a huge wool poncho, gesturing wildly as he spoke his poems by heart, Bly toured the country as a cultural guerrilla, haranguing his auditors on the various menaces plaguing American life. The poetry grew more violent, the presence of the poet more theatrical (and more intimately human, i.e., nonliterary), the political commitment more overt and militant. By the mid-1970s he'd become a counterculture hero, his face often gracing the covers of New Age publications.

Bly is established now; he appears on TV talk shows not only as a bardic personality but as a public spokesman for (of all things) "inwardness." A man of many paradoxes, Bly spends most of his time in relative seclusion on his Minnesota farm. Three times a year he goes on tour in order to stay home writing the rest of the year. He knows the hazards of being a public figure and writes of them with a wise perspective on the illusory nature of his own prominence. He understands that "talking, we do not say what we are," yet earns his living talking, turning people on and in to their private silences.

Responding to a San José newspaper headline describing him as "flamboyant," Bly remarked: "In the state of things today, if a person isn't entirely dead he's considered flamboyant." Actually Bly is considerably less outrageous and challenging than he used to be a few years back when he deliberately set out to make his audience squirm by probing their fear and guilt and rage as well as their more delicate sensitivities. Still, he's very much alive and working on his listeners on subtler and perhaps more dangerous levels of awareness.

Bly's dangerousness now arises from his presence as a benevolent, albeit lively, patriarch. The fatherly authority with which he speaks of writing and the psyche's inner dynamics seems to be swallowed whole-hog by most of his admirers, who—seeing him rightly as a carrier of *life*—may fail to note that many of the master's sweeping generalizations are not only inconsistent but unsupportable.

Claiming, for example, that the prose poem is more effective than the verse poem for addressing the mundane details of life, Bly ignores volumes of evidence to the contrary—beginning with the meticulously "ordinary" lyrics of William Carlos Williams and ending (I hope) with the manufactured boredom of the drivel currently emanating from college writing programs and countless unimaginative magazines. Since Rubén Darío of Nicaragua pioneered the form at the turn of the century (preceded by Baudelaire's and Rimbaud's prose poems and followed by other French and Hispanic surrealists), the modern prose poem has been a vehicle for exploring the baroque and visionary unknown more than for depicting the everyday.

Despite—or maybe on account of—such holes in his discourse, Bly is for real: he's no mere masquerader in the art of words. Poetry is a profession which engages the entire being of the artist; the poet's body and conduct as well as his or her mind should perpetually express the truth of a life lived consciously and always changing in reliably unpredictable directions.

At the moment, according to Bly, the *spoken* aspect of poetry is regaining its former significance over the printed page. The poem was once transmitted by the voice of the poet/singer without any written text, given from the heart and lungs of the bard by memory or spontaneously composed: a live performance.

As a bearer and resurrector of the oral tradition, Bly—his hair snow white, his face sparkling with age—will get along famously with or without his glasses. What strikes me as disturbing is the unquestioning passivity of his fans and acolytes. Unless they get out from under the hypnotic radiance of their master and discover some contradictory truths for themselves, all the poetry in the world won't rescue them from the drone of cultural consumption and the artificial glow of secondhand understanding.

1982

2 *The Accidental Televangelist*

Until his recent reading in Santa Cruz, Robert Bly had earned my gratitude for his tremendous contribution to American poetry over the last half century. Through his magazine *The Fifties*, later *The Sixties* and *The Seventies*, his poems and essays in other publications, his prolific translations of international poets and his polemical arguments for and against various trends in contemporary poetry, he played a role for us younger writers not unlike the one Ezra Pound had played for his generation—that of irascible teacher, explainer, provocateur and know-it-all blowhard. Bly livened things up for everyone, and inspired many of us to embrace our vocation with passionate commitment and independence.

It had been about twenty-five years since I'd last seen Bly in person, and despite his best-selling deviation into leadership of the "men's movement" in the 1980s and 1990s—his book *Iron John* and his weekend retreats where men would beat drums and emote about their lousy fathers and other misfortunes of growing up male in America—I still felt rather affectionate toward him, so I wanted to hear him one more time while I had the chance. Bly is a robust eighty and could last for many years yet, but you never know.

I'd first heard him read in 1967 when I was an undergraduate at Bard, and had watched his permutations over the years through many subsequent performances, from the conservatively dressed Midwestern pastoralist through the poncho-draped mask-deploying flamboyantly gesticulating confrontational antiwar poet to the somewhat mellower dulcimer-strumming but still provocative avuncular figure he was when I last saw him. Since then he'd become a mass-market guru of masculinity, but what the heck, he could always be trusted to put on a good show.

Tonight, forty years since that evening at Bard, the Santa Cruz club The Attic was packed, and the stage bedecked with a couple of giant Buddha faces whose constantly changing colors told me this must be a "multimedia" event. Since the Beat era some bards have been jazzing up their readings with various kinds of music—a gesture in the direction of poetry's origins as an oral and musical art—but how Bly's backup musicians on the Indian instruments of tabla and sarod would relate to his Norwegian-American poetry was anybody's guess.

As usual, the great man was charming, obnoxious, funny, overbearing, self-deprecating, grandfatherly and demagogic by turns. As a way of infantilizing his audience he asked straight off how many had a teacher (or perhaps a Teacher) and encouraged anyone without one to get one—implicitly volunteering his own pedagogical services to those in the crowd unfortunate enough to be teacherless. (I once heard the Dalai Lama say that your enemy is your teacher.) As the evening progressed the teacher-poet grew increasingly "spiritual" in his discourse and selection of poems, until by the reading's final offerings a couple of hours later, he was more like a New Age preacher, even cajoling the congregation into a poem-along—and they obediently submitted as to any other charismatic cult leader, sounding out the final word of his ersatz ghazals, which in the most egregious case was "Amen."

I couldn't help wondering if, had this been, say, George W. Bush giving a heartfelt pitch for his born-again Christianity, the public would have responded with such enthusiasm. Leaving aside the fact that Bly earlier in the evening had remarked that our grandchildren will ask us why we didn't shoot the president when we had the chance, the poet tonight was turning himself into a grotesque imitation of the evangelical proselytizers he presumably opposes.

It was also disturbing, not to say disgusting, to realize that the great iconoclast had become not only a geezerly icon but some sort of faith-based mountebank, a charlatan of the most shameless kind. Bly's recipe for spiritual wisdom is a half-baked concoction of Sufism and Hinduism and fairy tales and Christianity and Jungian psychology and Buddha-knows-what-all-else, but whatever it is it reeks of intellectual sloppiness and dishonesty.

As for the poetry, it was hard to tell, because the poet insisted on interrupting himself every few lines to explain to the ignorant masses what those lines were about, then repeating them two or three times just to be sure we got the message—and then repeating the whole poem, as if we really needed to hear it again—and of course each poem was followed by sighs and applause. But the actual experience of hearing a poem spoken in its integrity and entirety, and speaking for itself without the benefit of the poet's patronizing commentary, was sorely missing, and this distortion of the lyric art into a platform for pontificating on some incoherent quasi-religious doctrine was, for this witness, almost unbearable.

One of the unintentionally funniest things Bly said, and his second incitement to reckless gunplay, was that people should go home and shoot their television sets—as if TV and not the Internet were what is currently sucking people's brains out of their heads and keeping them from reading books—and I couldn't help marveling at how out of touch the old man is with contemporary culture.

And then there was the embarrassing nationalism of Bly's declaration that American poetry of the last forty years makes British and Canadian poets look dull by comparison. This may or may not be true—and how about Australian and Caribbean and Irish and other Anglophone poetry of our time?—but the gratuitousness of this kind of jingoistic flag-waving was worthy of any right-wing Republican.

How disappointing and depressing it is to see that in his old age Robert Bly has devolved into the Pat Robertson, the Deepak Chopra, the Oprah Winfrey, the Jim Jones of poetry. I still feel grateful for what he's done, but I'm not drinking any of his Kool-Aid.

2007

Moving Target:
Merwin's Elusive Music

Seated onstage in an armchair at Herbst Theater in San Francisco, W. S. Merwin looks relaxed. Legs crossed casually, crown of white hair radiant under the lights, Merwin is clearly comfortable in the role of distinguished man of letters as he deftly fields the questions of designated interlocutor Renee Rothmann of City Arts & Lectures in what is billed as a California Academy of Sciences Conversation. Sciences? Well, it's Earth Day, April 22, National Poetry Month, and in addition to his eminence as a poet and translator Merwin's environmentalist credentials are impeccable, cultivating as he does what is no doubt the planet's most famous "garden of rare and endangered palm trees" at his home on Maui. So he's here to discuss not only literature but nature, and maybe a bit of politics too, given his recent public denunciations of President George W. Bush and his policies in a much-circulated statement for Poets Against the War.

Now seventy-five and at the peak of a more than fifty-year career, turning out books of poetry, prose and translation at a pace that only accelerates with age, charmingly avuncular and sprightly at the same time, Merwin cuts an attractive yet unapproachable figure, his tenor voice smooth and melodic as a Ben Webster saxophone solo, his demeanor cool yet warm, serious yet witty, low-key, twinkly eyed, modest reserve recurrently broken by the subtle trace of something like a smirk—his signature expression, mischievous and maybe a little smug. One can hardly fault him for this attitude of evident self-satisfaction: he's published more than forty books and won nearly every prize of any consequence.

Yet given his towering stature, something about this evening is out of joint. The spacious hall is barely two-fifths full, and while nearly four hundred people is a respectable turnout for such an event, I had expected, as in the past, a sold-out crowd to hear this poet's poet. San Francisco after all has one of the more dynamic poetry communities in the country. But perhaps its billing as a science program, the eighteen-dollar ticket price (sure to discourage low-budget bohemians), the exodus from the city of many writerly and artistic types during the dot-com boom of the nineties, a freshly depressed economy, low-grade terrorism scares, and the fact that this isn't a reading but an interview have all combined to keep away a larger cross-section of the literati. Despite his fame in literary circles, Merwin has managed to maintain an almost invisible public profile—unlike such poetry stars as Billy Collins and Maya Angelou—and his deliberate abstention from celebrity may be another factor in the failure to fill the house.

But I can't help thinking of another aspect of Merwin's prodigious career that may have contributed to the number of empty seats. Since being anointed by W. H. Auden the Yale Younger Poet of 1952 (when that award was virtually the only one of its kind and either the launching pad or the kiss of death for a bard on the way up) Merwin has been such a constant presence in American poetry that it's easy to take him for granted, like some monumental feature of the natural landscape. He writes books faster than most people can read them, and his name turns up in the respectable highbrow and progressive press (*The New Yorker*, *The New York Review*, *The Nation*, *The New York Times Book Review*, *The American Poetry Review* and countless other journals) almost as often as that of the ubiquitous John Updike. Thankfully, Merwin lacks Updike's smarmy glibness, but in terms of sheer production he's comparably phenomenal; so perhaps it's that omnipresence in print that makes his appearance in this poetry mecca too routine to cause much of a ripple.

Still, those of us who've shown up to hear him are getting our money's worth, as Rothman's questions are evocative enough to get the great man talking. She opens with an Earth Day reference to his "palm tree forest," and he seems flattered by the designation but corrects her: "We don't know how to make forests. Forests make forests. We know how to plant trees." He explains that the depleted state of his land has required years of corrective cultivation, and from there digresses into a discourse on natural ecosystems and how they're composed of multitudes of species interrelating in webs of interconnection too complex to be replicated by anything man-made. This strikes me as an apt metaphor for Merwin's literary career, the fertile interaction of his original poetry with translation from several languages (sometimes working with other scholars) and various forms of prose (fictions, memoir, essays, criticism) amounting to a kind of artistic ecosystem in which no individual element can be separated out from the others without diminishing the integrity of the whole.

As a translator alone Merwin's contribution has been immense, from his versions of such contemporaries as Jaime Sabines (Mexico) and Roberto Juarroz (Argentina) to the resurrection of such classical epics as *Poem of the Cid* and Dante's *Purgatorio*, and beyond Romance languages, from collaborations on Osip Mandelstam through Sanskrit love lyrics to renderings of little zingers from various East Asian languages and cultures. His translations are characterized by a lightness of touch, a graceful ability to stay out of the original's way while attempting to convey its meaning and a trace of its music—unlike some other translators who, consciously or not, tend to interpose their own personalities between the original and the reader. "What fascinated me about poetry as a child was hearing differences in the language," he says in response to a question on how he got started. "Poetry is not like prose," it is "a different kind of language," and from early on he set out to explore those differences.

A visit to Ezra Pound when Merwin was nineteen proved formative. Pound told him that if he was serious about poetry he should write seventy-five lines a day. Since nineteen-year-olds don't have much experience of their own to write about, Pound advised: "Translate, you will learn your own language." (Merwin noted as an aside that if he had known at the time about Pound's politics—the old man was imprisoned in a Washington, DC, mental hospital for his pro-fascist ravings on Italian radio during World War II—he wouldn't have gone to see him. Now, he added, he'd go to see him in spite of his politics.)

While Pound's bizarre and often noxious political and economic theories frequently infected his poetry, Merwin has very seldom written explicitly political poems. His longtime commitment to pacifism has manifested in other forms—like counseling draft resisters during the Vietnam era, writing a letter to *The New York Times* in January 2001 denouncing the stolen presidential election, and publishing his even more scathingly critical "Statement" for Poets Against the War. His political prose is forceful, precise and economical, but it is indeed a different kind of language from his verse, which tends to be enigmatic and ambiguous. "The poem should come first," he says. "That's one of the problems with political poetry. That's why most political poetry is so bad. You know what you're trying to say. You're trying to persuade somebody."

His environmentalism is easier to detect in the poems because his regard for nature is suffused with religious awe, a humble reverence for the cryptic workings of the elements. Apart from such nearly satirical poems as "Questions to Tourists Stopped by a Pineapple Field," or fabulist parables like "The Last One," Merwin's take on landscapes tends to be both specific and archetypal, precisely descriptive of places where he's lived (France, Mexico, Hawaii) yet at the same time strangely elemental, as if these mountains and trees and rivers and animals exist purely in some universal consciousness of which the poet is merely a medium. The heart of Merwin's lyric verse resides in a sense of immanence—as in Hawaiian myth, where the natural landscape, as he says in San Francisco, "*is* the gods, not representations of the gods." This surely relates to his Buddhism, but he nimbly deflects a question about his own religious practice by citing the Hawaiian archetypes invoked in his epic *The Folding Cliffs*. It's a tasteful way of avoiding any claim to spiritual authority or enlightenment, and typical of Merwin's cagey evasiveness when it comes to revealing too much of his personal self.

That a core thematic element of his most intimate lyric verse should also inform his most ambitious historical narrative poem only serves to illustrate the ecosystemic interconnectedness of everything he writes. And if one were to think, on the basis of what I've said, that Merwin is merely or mainly some kind of tree-hugging pastoralist, you would have to ignore his numerous vivid evocations of urban experience in such poems as "The Crossroads of the World Etc.," "St. Vincent's," "The Plumbing," or the more recent and deeply nostalgic "227 Waverly Place" and "Sixth Floor Walk-Up." For many years Merwin kept an apartment in Greenwich Village and spent about half his time there. His New York City poems are some of his finest, in the same way the best of his nature poems resound in multiple registers: the specificity of perception is closely entwined with a sense of cosmic mystery, so that no matter how precisely evoked a particular streetscape or sensory mixture of urban sights and sounds—the rich Whitmanic multiplicity of the actual city with its wealth of human solitudes—there's always a sense of some truth or understanding that's just beyond reach, a feeling of comprehension we never (as poet or reader) are able to grasp. It's this intangible quality, this elusive fluidity of awareness and expression that gives these texts their hypnotic power and invites us back in to read them again and again.

Fluidity—it's not just *The River Sound* or *The Rain in the Trees* (to cite the watery titles of two of his books) that give his poems their elemental slipperiness but the physical construction of the verse itself running along unpunctuated with only line breaks or extra spaces to indicate caesuras, or pauses, or eddies in the flow of the song. Merwin's mastery of prosody, his uncanny control of poetic technique, has been evident from the beginning—it seems to be half the point of his early poems, many of which now read like rhetorical exercises designed to impress his teachers with their formal elegance and classical décor. Then, about halfway through his fifth book, *The Moving Target* (1963), punctuation begins to evaporate until, in his next collection, *The Lice* (1967), one of the landmark books of its era, scarcely a comma can be found. He has since gone on to purify his technique to resemble, as he put it in an interview, the nailless construction of some traditional Japanese buildings, notching his lines so precisely and seamlessly that the weight and rhythm of the words themselves are held in a natural equilibrium that is in fact the result of extremely sophisticated artifice. The poems, made purely of words, at times have the feel of subverbal thought-streams, preconscious apprehensions of reality mysteriously seeping into speech. Yet the deeper you go into their obscurity, the clearer they get. (To write without clarity, Merwin says, is "bad manners.")

His facility with both traditional forms and those of his own invention, the subtlety with which he sustains syllabic structures and patterns of rhyme, make most of the "neoformalists" look like amateurs; but beyond this technical virtuosity, and its deployment to suggest what is ultimately inexpressible, it is the metaphysical aspect of Merwin's work that may be its most pervasive characteristic. In San Francisco, for example, he speaks of "all the different ways in which time is a fiction."

This leads him to the Heraclitean observation: "The creation is happening even as it's happened. At the same time. Everything is always beginning." Like this statement, many of his poems dwell less on particular images than metaphysical principles in progress, states of awareness working themselves out, thought in pursuit of the ineffable. Resisting the comfort of neat conclusions, declining to draw lessons or offer instruction, Merwin's best poems embody the poignancy and pathos of human ignorance. One of the few consolations we have, he implies, is the music (or poetry, as the case may be) with which to lament our lack of understanding.

If this sounds excessively pessimistic, I would argue that it's more a kind of mystical skepticism, a surrender to or immersion in the incomprehensible combined with a constantly questioning discontent that refuses to take anything for an answer. And it isn't just in the poetry that this questioning occurs. One of Merwin's most amazing books, *The Miner's Pale Children* (1970)—as well as its companion volume *Houses and Travellers* (1977)—explores in brief prose fables or parables many of the same thematic preoccupations that run throughout his poems. Neither stories in any conventional sense, nor essays, nor prose poems, nor "tales" exactly, the prose in these books appears to be yet another instrument the writer has devised in order both to examine and embody the largely metaphysical questions (as in "Unchopping a Tree" or "Where Laughter Came From") that lines of verse could never quite account for. These strange proses defy description because they themselves are impossibly successful attempts to describe the indescribable.

Even in his more conventional books of prose—the memoiristic portraits of *Unframed Originals*, the regional narratives of *The Lost Upland*, the medieval literary history disguised as travel guide in *The Mays of Ventadorn*—Merwin's writing subverts existing genres. It is as if he is compelled to reinvent whatever form he puts his hand to, in this way honoring the absence of definition that is in some sense his philosophical signature. Only in his critical writings does he sound anything like a normal practitioner of the genre he's chosen (the book review, for example), and even then his particular intelligence and unusual turn of mind tend to give his insights and arguments a distinctly Merwinian twist. It's true, of course, that any writer evolves characteristic idiosyncrasies, but in Merwin's case it's all the more surprising, after the weirdness of his imaginative inventions, to hear him sound like the erudite scholar and sober critic he also is.

It's worth noting here that, unlike most American poets of his own and subsequent generations, Merwin has somehow managed to make a career as a writer without ever taking a job in academia. Perhaps part of his singularity has to do with having steered clear not just of universities but schools of poetry as well. While identified by some with the "deep image" poets of the sixties and seventies, he's never been associated with any group or movement, has managed to outmaneuver his imitators by frequently changing styles even while maintaining an unmistakable voice, and has remained largely above and beyond the various esthetic and ideological altercations among American poets over the last half century, patiently and relentlessly proceeding with his own project. At the same time, in recent years especially, he has judged contests, sat as a chancellor of the Academy of American Poets, written blurbs for books of the lesser known, and accepted the various honors that have steadily come his way. In short, he has remained outside all the mainstreams, keeping to himself while still participating in the literary community, a loner with a sense of social obligation.

"One of the things that makes poetry different from prose is that a poem is physical," Merwin says. "If you don't *hear* poetry you don't get it." He speaks of the necessity, for both poet and reader, of "learning how to listen" and "suddenly hearing something." I believe what he's talking about here is a quality of attention crucial not only to the act of composition and the pleasures of appreciation but to a way—a specifically "poetic" way—of being in the world. One needs to be receptive in order to be creative. You must allow the information, the music, the river of language to flow through you in order to find the inspiration that informs the active work of the artist. Composure, discipline, humility are required in the service of something greater than yourself.

At the end of the evening an audience member asks Merwin to describe the relation between his writing and his person, to explain how it is in his experience that a poem comes into being. "I don't know," he replies, "and I don't want to know. I think that poetry comes out of something you don't know. And the unknown is all around us. It's inexhaustible."

2003

Frank O'Hara:
A Painter's Poet

Brilliant, bitchy, prolific, promiscuous, hyperactive, charismatic, alcoholic, Frank O'Hara was a major force in the New York artistic renaissance of the 1950s and 1960s. Intimately interconnected by love, friendship and esthetics with the Abstract Expressionist painters of the time, O'Hara lived at the hot center of an unusually fertile moment in US cultural history; like García Lorca in Spain some thirty years earlier, the American poet was a living inspiration to his contemporaries, a key presence in a collective creative upsurge, and like Lorca he died suddenly in his prime.

Well, perhaps he was past his prime, if biographer Brad Gooch is right. According to Gooch's good and gossipy book, *City Poet*, Hara's poetic powers were in decline by 1966 when one night on Fire Island he was run over by a beach buggy. He was forty years old. The gradual reduction of his prodigious poetic output appears to have been due to a combination of a demanding career as a curator at the Museum of Modern Art—mounting shows of American painters all over Europe as well as in New York—and a drunken social life that never let up. After peaking in the early sixties and eventually gaining renown in the literary/artistic underground and beyond, the poet's writing began to sputter even as his legend grew.

Even before his death O'Hara's style was widely imitated by the next generation of urbane bards. His influence—via his frankly autobiographical yet lightly surreal approach to the poem, his talky lyricism, a spontaneous playful gift for putting even the most mundane information into the work and somehow making it mythic gossip—was liberating to many younger writers. It spawned a certain amount of lightweight O'Haraese among the lesser acolytes, but for those with authentic voices of their own O'Hara's example led them deeper into their natural instincts. Perhaps Jack Kerouac was right when, at a New York reading, he heckled, "O'Hara, you're ruining American poetry." But O'Hara's snappy reply, "That's more than you ever did," is typical of the quick wit and ironic intelligence that sparkle throughout his verse.

And what poems they are—the nervous buoyancy, the hip yet almost pastoral romanticism applied to life on the streets and in the studios of the city, the speed of association, the range of reference from private jokes to pop iconography (O'Hara's elegies for James Dean and Billie Holiday still send chills through the reader) to highbrow art-historical and musical allusions, the passion for friendship and for sexual connection—his five-hundred page *Collected Poems* is a volume phenomenal not only for its weight but for its wealth of laughs and gasps and tears. Openly gay, free with his love, obsessively drawn to straight painters, male and female, and to beautiful younger men who served as his muses, O'Hara seems never to have found much peace or lasting satisfaction in romance. But the tension of desire and the interpersonal complications of an incestuous multi-sexual circle give much of his best writing its electricity.

An understanding of community is vital to appreciating O'Hara's art. The all-star assortment of outstanding poets hitting their stride in New York at the time—John Ashbery, Kenneth Koch, LeRoi Jones, James Schuyler, Barbara Guest, Edward Field, Diane di Prima, Allen Ginsberg (though more often associated with the San Francisco Beat scene, Ginsberg always kept a foot in Manhattan)—many of whom would mingle socially with vanguard visual artists such as Jackson Pollock, Willem de Kooning, Robert Motherwell, Jane Freilicher, Grace Hartigan, Larry Rivers and many others—made for a substantial amount of mutual inspiration. O'Hara's poems are studded with dedications and nods to his pals and peers, and Gooch's biography places many of these references in the context of the poet's hectic party-going and tumultuous love life.

Which is all very interesting, of course. What's missing in *City Poet* is a deeper reading not only of the poems but the art criticism O'Hara did which made explicit his esthetic affinities with his painterly soul mates. Excerpts from these writings, or at least a summary of their central ideas, would have enriched this portrait, but Gooch seems content to focus on the scene rather than interpret his subject's thought.

"Personism," O'Hara's mock-manifesto banged out one day in 1959 as a statement on poetics for Donald Allen's landmark anthology *The New American Poetry 1945–1960,* for all its satiric flippancy does sort of summarize his writing strategy in typically O'Haraesque terms. Eschewing abstract theories of composition, he declares: "You just go on your nerve. If someone's chasing you down the street with a knife you just run, you don't turn around and shout, 'Give it up! I was a track star for Mineola Prep' …As for measure and other technical apparatus, that's just common sense: if you're going to buy a pair of pants you want them to be tight enough so everyone will want to go to bed with you." Personism, he earnestly explains, "has nothing to do with philosophy, it's all art…one of its minimal aspects is to address itself to one person (other than the poet himself), thus evoking overtones of love without destroying love's life-giving vulgarity, and sustaining the poet's feelings towards the poem while preventing love from distracting him into feeling about the person…The poem is at last between two persons instead of two pages."

Gooch's pages remind the reader of the powerful personality that drove the poetry's creation. It's a most singular and winning personality, for all its manic self-destructive energies. What finally commands our interest, though, is less the life as reported by the biographer than the one recorded in the poems. While the testimony of O'Hara's friends and lovers is often illuminating, the most compelling evidence of the poet's day-to-day genius is his poetry, which remains as fresh and as full of surprises as ever.

1993

Baraka and Back

No one in the United States writes with greater emotional intensity and stylistic snap than Amiri Baraka. At fifty, Baraka—formerly known as LeRoi Jones—is one of the most versatile, prolific and controversial American writers, author of dozens of books of poetry, essays, plays and fiction, editor of magazines and anthologies, community organizer, political agitator, literary hero and villain to thousands of readers who, whatever else they may think of him, can't deny his power.

Baraka reads live in the oral/musical mode, blowing rhythmic riffs straight out of bebop fused with literate cinematic crosscutting, dashes of salsa, basketball-court razzing of real and imagined adversaries, lucid articulations of the urban scream. His presence in performance shows like no book ever could the electrifying force of the spoken word brandished with passion. Even without hearing him, however, one can feel the juice in his verse and prose because the mind at work there is always *moving*.

Baraka has earned enemies because he swings to extremes as a political philosopher and polemicist, renouncing his former friends and selves in hair-raising lyrical exorcisms and excoriating enemies with tongue-lashings the likes of which you haven't heard since your most paranoid nightmares. A casual tour through his early-to-middle work reveals a fair amount of Jew-baiting, woman-hating, fag-bashing, ofay-trashing and other forms of verbal abuse seemingly unworthy of a great spirit; but in manifesting artistically his changing rage Baraka has given creative shape to generations of American black male anger.

Young black artists must come to terms with Baraka's song and thought precisely because of his extremist energy, stirring up troublesome consciousness nonstop since the early sixties. His essays on African-American cultural history, especially the music known as blues and jazz, are essential reading for anyone seeking to understand the social meaning of these indigenous artforms. Experiencing his poetry, plays and stories, readers and writers of whatever color can pick up insights into the making of a painfully personal voice which speaks a collective language.

Early in 1984 Baraka brought out *The Autobiography of LeRoi Jones*, a prose narrative which attempts to track from the beginning the impressions, confusions, mad dashes, switchbacks, revelations, twists, collisions and resurrections of a life lived daredevil-style on the streets of Newark, New Jersey, through Howard University and the United States Air Force, to Greenwich Village, Harlem and back to Newark as a born-again homeboy sharpening the edge of a Marxist ax at forty after embracing, developing and rejecting various other fanaticisms en route.

Describing his boyhood style as a playground athlete, Baraka reveals a scrappy pattern evident throughout his life and writing: "I would fight, do anything to stop losing. I would play super-hard, attacking, with endless energy, to stop a loss. I would shout and drive my team on. Stick my hands in the opponents' faces, guard them chest to chest, or slash through the line from the backfield and catch them as they got the pass back from center. Or take the passes and cut around end and streak for the goal. Or double-step, skip, stop, leap, jump back, ram, twist, hop, back up, duck, get away, hustle, and rush into the end zone...I would slide head first into home, even first. On tar and cement. I would turn bunts into home runs, by just putting my head down and raging around the bases."

Streetcorner jive, the dozens, the blues, the "high speech" recently evolved as rap, "with everything at stake, even your ass"—all these oral urban traditions can be heard in everything Baraka has written, from the early anguished introspective lyrics to the latest flat-out diatribes. "How to rhyme. How to reach in your head to its outermost reaches. How to invent and create." Fusing these popular modes with an astute sense of jazz improvisation and a highly sophisticated literary modernism nourished by Joyce and William Carlos Williams and his own contemporaries, young LeRoi Jones emerged in Greenwich Village in the late fifties and early sixties as the brightest black light on the literary scene, scorching the eyelashes of the avant-garde with his white-hot artistry.

Coming of age among a wave of poets who opened new paths of wild and exact poetic expression—Allen Ginsberg, Frank O'Hara, Robert Creeley, Denise Levertov, Gary Snyder and others—Baraka, married to a white woman and surrounded by white bohemians, was some kind of spicy olive in a martini not of his own making. Following the success of his play *Dutchman*, the contradictions between his people's plight and his new-found New York celebrity were skewering him with self-hate. You can see it eating him alive in his poetry, first in *The Dead Lecturer* (1964) and turning outward in the direction of a despised Whitey in *Black Magic* (1968). A sensitive young man, tormented by his times, messed up in search of integrity, overly talented, craving justice, lashes his phantoms in these books, seeking a way out of self-betrayal.

As if his 1960 trip to Cuba weren't enough, Baraka writes that the assassination of Malcolm X in 1965 brought home to him how out of place he was bopping around downtown while up in Harlem the brothers and sisters of his blood were suffering in the chains of an enslaved culture. He moved uptown and founded the Black Arts Repertory Theater/School, a neighborhood cultural center which brought African-American drama, music, painting, poetry and politics into the street as forms of "an art that would reach the people, that would take them higher, ready them for war and victory, as popular as the Impressions or the Miracles or Marvin Gaye." Black Arts became an arm of cultural rebellion and identity which fed and was informed by the Black Liberation Movement on the political front, as one after another American ghettos were going up in flames.

Through both his writing and his organizing, LeRoi Jones became a major mover not only in New York but in the national black (and Black Nationalist) consciousness. White folks who dared could discover a great deal of what was going on among Afro-Americans by diving into such books as *Tales, Home* and *Blues People*. What they found there was often disturbing, especially to liberals bent on befriending the Negro. White help suddenly was not wanted. In its rejection of the white esthetic and European cultural values the Black Arts movement came to be labeled "racist."

"So strange," writes Baraka in *The Autobiography*, "that the victims, once they began to scream and shout at their oppressors, can now be termed the oppressors. We accuse whites of racism, so—Presto! Chango!—'black racism' is the real problem…

"We had no stated ideology except 'black,' and that meant many things to many people, much of it useful, much of it not. But we shot from the hip, came always off the top or near the top of our heads. Our sincerity was our real ideology, a gestalt of our experience, an eclectic mixture of what we thought we knew and understood. What we wanted. Who we thought we were. It was very messy." So messy, in fact, that internal tensions and personality conflicts and power trips split up the Black Arts project within a year, sending Baraka-to-be back home to Newark, where soon he began new and continuing efforts of cultural agitation.

In the nearly twenty years since his return to Newark, Baraka has remained at the front lines as an artistic warrior, going through various ideological permutations—the latest of which is "Marxist–Leninist–Mao Tse Tung thought"—but always in motion, maintaining a fervor and a fierce commitment that get under people's skin. As Greg Tate points out in *The Village Voice* (October 2, 1984), Baraka throughout his career has had a remarkable knack for projecting his personal conflicts and "mental problems" onto the outside world as historic facts, responding to every internal crisis in such a way that it becomes a public event. Conversely, he takes public events personally. It is this integration—some would say confusion—of private and public worlds in all his work, wrought through his dazzling linguistic craft, which gives his words the urgency of action.

And action is what his work in Newark has been about, both in the arts and in local politics, writing increasingly militant poetry (which many of his former admirers consider inferior to his earlier work but which moves and raves with the same supercharged wit and an even greater oral/aural clarity, attuned to the news of black speech in all its musical flexibility) and campaigning at every level for community institutions which serve that city's majority. It is impossible to separate Baraka's art from his politics, not because he's obsessed or pathological—though certainly in his most inspired moments he writes as one *possessed*—but because he functions as a whole person, bringing his inner convictions to bear on everything he does.

People who expect such absolute truths from the man as he may imagine himself to be speaking, moment to moment, might take a step back for a panoramic gander at the sweep and range of his creative thought in order to see his development as a dialectical process which keeps on contradicting itself in the course of provoking others. By presenting his own story and stormy ideas for public scrutiny, Baraka may sometimes play the role of the fool but he never bores his audience. More often his scholarship and commitment cut through to the essential arguments, slashing the fat from the American language. In his mouth even the most rhetorical exhortations come irritatingly alive.

Like any red-blooded revolutionary, Amiri Baraka wants to change the world, and has gone about it by changing himself, over and over again. Having settled in Newark with a homegirl/woman and raised a family while carrying on with his public struggles, he seems to have established a steadier pattern in recent years than in his brilliantly volatile youth. *The Autobiography* adds important testimony to the body of Baraka's work, revealing the links between his personal tale and the historic changes that have engaged him. The "misunderstanding and mistakes" he acknowledges only serve to humanize his prodigious accomplishments on the paths of art and activism.

1984

Wendell Berry,
Resident on Earth

Trying to talk about Wendell Berry is risky business. The temptation is to call him "the sanest man in America" or some equally convenient and misplaced media superlative. He emanates good sense.

Comparisons to Thoreau and Emerson are obvious, only Berry is a better poet than either of them and, because he works with his hands farming full time, he's also a wiser philosopher. The rhythms of wholesome physical work suffuse Berry's words and give them a convincing resonance. In the groundedness of his language one feels the integrity of meticulous practical know-how and an attention attuned to slowly growing things. He is a radical—that is, truly rooted—thinker.

But to turn him into another New Age eco-hero or icon of the organic to be consumed with Carlos Castaneda and the rest of the mental health foods on the market is to betray what Berry stands for. If he is a hero it is because he is an ordinary man keeping himself and his family alive the best way he knows how, which is by farming.

Good farming—the source of most human nutrition—is

the model by which Berry measures the health of a culture; a durable, self-renewing agriculture is a vital sign. That he happens to be gifted with graceful language makes Berry an ideal medium for transmitting the spiritual and moral values of sound agricultural practice.

Literature, after all, is a kind of agriculture of the spirit: a farming of human speech for its most nutritious and suggestive resonances, meanings, sounds and flavors. Poems and stories need to be crafted to last if they're to have cultural value. For culture is partly collective memory, and if language gets shoddy that memory will drift.

The word *pattern* keeps recurring in Berry's writing. By pattern he means relationships of details—in an ecosystem, for instance—which interconnect in continuous harmony and health. Farming, for Berry, is closely akin to music.

But it has nothing to do with entertainment. The farmer who farms carelessly or poorly is putting people's lives (and his own livelihood) on the line—if not now, in the next generation or the one after. As agriculture is currently practiced in the United States, topsoil is being virtually stripmined— eroded, compacted or otherwise poisoned—by mechanized petroleum-dependent corporate practices which render food as a mass-production commodity rather than as the sacrament of humankind's relation to the earth.

At the rate agribusiness is depleting the very source of food—the topsoil—the United States could be in for some serious starvation within a century. It is the sobering prospect of a food-free future and the complexity of its possible solutions that make Berry's books and his speech so compelling.

Living outside the network of dependencies and addictions

most of us take for granted, working with horses his seventy-five acres of Kentucky hillside (in the county where his family has farmed for generations), Berry has a clearheaded perspective on the nature of the sick beast of these States. *The Unsettling of America* is the most profound and sensible analysis of our current predicament that I have read. If food is the basis of human life, how that food is produced has a lasting effect on human society. Intelligent farming is a matter of life and death.

During his visit to Santa Cruz last week in connection with the appearance of his new book of essays, *The Gift of Good Land*, Berry gave a talk entitled "People, Land and Community." North Point Press (his publisher) and Writers and Poets in Santa Cruz, the sponsors of the event, didn't anticipate having to turn away the fifty or a hundred extra people who couldn't be squeezed into the hall. The man appears to have a following—and it's a little unsettling to think of him becoming popular.

But Berry is protected by his strangeness from the hazards of celebrity. So far he seems immune to hero worship. He speaks with real humility because he can't be fooled by his own eloquence into believing he knows anything. Life is an endless mystery in which we can participate most joyfully by learning to work in the service of the land that feeds us. "Nature is never in a hurry," says Berry. If we are to survive we must help the soil build its fertility, just as we must allow "essential wisdom" to accumulate in communities through the ongoing interconnectedness of people, land and work.

In Berry's poetry and prose, as in his talk, there is a reverence riddled with a salty recognition of how difficult it is to be a human being. "As humans," he points out, "we not only *have* problems but *are* problems." Fielding a question from the audience about the ethics of eating meat, he replied: "You know, the fix that we're in is that we can't live but at the expense of somethin'—plants or animals, one. Or both."

Living well requires skills, it requires work and it requires respect for the miracle of creation. The contempt with which industrial agriculture treats its livestock (a regimen of hormones and confinement feeding) and its land—eating the soil of its own acreage out from under itself—is a symptom of cultural corruption.

Culture for Berry is not "the Philharmonic" but a dance of practical, moral and spiritual relations woven into a community through time. Such a dance can occur only among a rooted citizenry. One reason American culture is unraveling is that our mobility—greatly accelerated by the automobile—has literally driven us away from our own past. We are still this much like the first immigrants: in our flight from what's behind us we can hardly see where we are for what it is.

No matter how many skyscrapers and art museums we erect, real culture depends on the recognition of how things *are* in nature and, within that, on the common skills of conscientious workmanship. In other words, "if people's buttons are sewed on right, the Philharmonic has a longer life expectancy."

Few machine-made artifacts can match the beauty and utility—and durability—of an artifact fashioned by human hands. The harmony of healthy culture amounts to moral law: a sense of limits and understood values cultivated for generations. Technology must be subjected to "the assessment and restraint of cultural value" if it is to be introduced without disrupting that harmony. The full-speed-ahead futurologists who expect advanced technology to solve all problems, fast, are making a grave mistake.

"If we want to get safely home," says Berry, "there are certain seductive songs we must not turn aside for." The inner strength, or character, of Homer's Odysseus—his very survival—hinges on his ability to restrain himself and his shipmates from the lure of the Sirens. For us, every "labor-saving device" and "technological breakthrough" is such an attempted seduction: a promise of easy life at no extra cost. But life is never easy and in fact responds generously only to patient and attentive husbandry—whether in marriage, livestock breeding, gardening or art.

Invoking the mud-daubers—black wasps that hum to the mud as they build their nests—as an example of harmony in work, Berry reveals a kernel of his own poetics: the insects are "mastering their material by a kind of song."

Yet it's not enough just to cultivate and serenade his own land. As a member of what's left—or beginning—of a human community, Berry, through his books and through lectures like the one he gave last week, brings the nourishing music of his thought into common air. How we transform such shapely insight into the matter of our daily lives may take lifetimes to discover, but Berry's steady voice reminds us where we have to begin looking.

1981

A Poetry Home Companion:
The Doglike Genius of **Billy Collins**

At nine o'clock on a Saturday morning last November, in a vast hall at the Sacramento Convention Center, I had the curious pleasure of hearing Billy Collins, keynote speaker of the California Library Association's annual conference, read his poems to a couple of thousand delighted librarians. It was the first time I had witnessed the Collins phenomenon in person, and it was edifying not so much for the poetry itself—which was predictably and charmingly Billyesque—as for the response of the audience, a presumably literate but not especially poetry-centric crowd, and therefore typical of this anomalously best-selling poet's readers and fans. They laughed at the funny parts, which were many, and after the end of every poem released a collective sigh, followed by grateful and sincerely sustained applause.

I expect I enjoyed this reading as much as anyone; the clarity, simplicity, wit and occasional poignancy of Collins's writing is irresistible, and his low-key, just-folks persona is pleasant, and in many ways far more engaging than the highfalutin, self-dramatizing, angst-riddled, neurotic, arrogant and/or intellectually pretentious poses assumed by many contemporary poets. And laughter is a valuable element in any truly serious undertaking. But applause has never struck me as an appropriate response to poetry, any more than one would be inclined to clap at a painting one found particularly moving. At the most powerful poetry readings there is a silence one hears at the end of poems that signals a depth of connection, a resonance, a spell that would only be broken by any sound so vulgar as applause. Of course there is also the dead silence of befuddlement, and any experienced poetry-goer knows the difference. "I saw the best minds of my generation destroyed by boredom at poetry readings," as Lawrence Ferlinghetti pointedly put it.

But Billy Collins is a crowd-pleaser, and this, self-evident as it may seem, is crucial to understanding both his mass appeal and his debasement of the art form he so winningly represents. After his CLA performance, I read his selected poems, *Sailing Alone Around the Room*, and his most recent book, *The Trouble with Poetry*, in hopes of discovering what it is about this writer that speaks to me and so many others, yet also annoys me in his calculated strategy of wholesale ingratiation. At his reading I kept imagining Collins as a dog—not the big scary kind that jumps up and knocks you over, or shoves his nose obnoxiously up your ass, but, say, a friendly little pooch who hops into your lap and licks your face, smiling and wagging his tail in such a way that you can't really get too angry at the transgression. This intuition of the poet as dog was confirmed when I read his books and discovered that he not only writes frequently about, but that he actually identifies, again and again, with dogs, and even sees one of his ideal (unwritten) poems as a dog, with "the little insight at the end / wagging like the short tail / of a perfectly obedient spaniel / sitting by the door."

Maybe I'm just a cat person, preferring my pets and poets cool and aloof, but to me there is something unseemly about such a blatant play for readerly approval. And this eagerness to please, alas, is the essence of Billy Collins. In Sacramento he spoke revealingly of "the neurosis of art," positing as a motive for the creative impulse the need to be loved by strangers. "Why would you want strangers to love you?" he asked rhetorically. Why indeed. Without getting too Freudian about it, I would argue that there's plenty of evidence to suggest that while many artists and writers may start out mainly wanting to get laid (which is not to be confused with being loved), there are deeper motivations at work in the greatest creators, and these seldom include kissing up to the audience. In literature, in music, in painting, in dance—especially in their more lyric manifestations—there is a drive to articulate or express the otherwise unsayable, the ineffable, to respond to experience with uncompromising honesty or transforming imagination, to communicate something true and not necessarily to make the audience, and thus the artist, feel good about himself.

I am as impatient as the next person with deliberate obfuscation masquerading as profundity, and with the inane antics of the neo-Ashberian wonderboys whose razzle-dazzle incoherence passes for postmodern sophistication, but some "difficult" poetry is difficult for a reason. It may be exploring complex or troubling realities and so must adopt a form, a voice, a style suitable to the density of its themes. It demands something of the reader, and offers in return a more enduring engagement, a journey into mystery or imaginative thinking that outlasts, say, a good joke. Collins at his best is a fine parodist, sending up venerable modes and forms with an insouciant irreverence that refreshes as it ridicules what it's satirizing—the funniest example of this may be his Borgesian invention of the "paradelle," which he describes in a footnote as "one of the more demanding French fixed forms" with a complicated set of rules that ends up, in his "Paradelle for Susan," randomly throwing leftover "the"s and "to"s into the last line of every rigorously composed stanza. But he is not unserious in his meticulous prosody, his finely calibrated tone and his occasional feint in the direction of the spooky or weird. Even his "simple" language is acutely self-conscious in its plainspokenness and in its use of startling turns of phrase and image.

But as the Random House copywriter brags on the jacket flap of *The Trouble with Poetry*, "Collins shows that good poetry doesn't have to traffic in obscurity or incomprehensibility—qualities that are perhaps the *real* trouble with most 'serious' poetry." Oh yeah? The trouble with most serious poetry, or most of anything, is that it's mediocre, not that it's incomprehensible—and incomprehensible to whom? Good poetry doesn't condescend, it doesn't have to spell itself out with a little moral or offer a predigested "insight" or teach a lesson or presume the stupidity of the reader and set out to flatter him or her by suggesting the poet is just like them, only more clever. Even Collins himself, in the title poem, doesn't complain about "serious" poetry but declares that "the trouble with poetry is / that it encourages the writing of more poetry." Which suggests either that he's worried about competition, concerned that he's only adding to the glut, or feels guilty that, as a teacher of poetry writing, he's spreading a virus that's already epidemic. One perusal of *Poets & Writers* magazine is enough to convince anyone that the trouble with poetry is its indiscriminate proliferation into an industry, and into countless "career" paths or paths to possible fame as a mass-market bard like Billy.

Maybe Collins goes by that boyish name in order to discourage people from taking him too seriously. He could just as easily have called himself, for professional purposes, William, or Bill, or Will, or W. S. (or whatever his middle initial may be). Billy—as in Billy the Kid—is a boy's name, in his case not that of a precocious outlaw but a good boy who only wants to please his parents and teachers and peers, and of course readers, with his wholesome cuteness, his puppy-like playfulness, his Billyness. The name, like everything else about Collins, is calculated to charm and disarm, one more element in his folksy persona, which may be in some way sincere but may also contain a subtext of contempt for those admirers naïve enough to take him at face value.

Celebrity, after all, can be a huge nuisance, and the combination of commercial success and critical acclaim that Collins has received creates a demand for more of the same—a death sentence for any artist who wants to remain creative. The prolific, practically mechanical benevolence with which he dishes out his comfort-food verses makes me wonder if he's really as pleased with himself as he appears to be. Just as George W. Bush's cocky obtuseness would be unobjectionable if he weren't president of the United States, Collins's shtick would be harmless if he weren't the most beloved poet in the country and therefore setting a standard of talented normality as the pinnacle of poetic achievement. He has actually created a metapoetics of the mundane; most of his poems are explicitly engaged in describing or examining the act, his *routine*, of writing—sitting at his table, looking out the window, listening to music, scribbling in his notebook, tapping at his typewriter, petting his dog, etc. His ironic, self-aware perspective on this process matches that of the most "experimental" or "postmodern" contemporaries, but Collins is proudly anti-intellectual even while being shrewdly cognizant of the traditions he's trying to subvert—mainly Modernism and Romanticism. As a little-known poet published by university presses, Collins was just another toiler in the fields of verse, free to surprise himself and a few readers, but now that he's a brand name he must meet the expectations of his fans or be destroyed—or worse, abandoned—by them.

This evolution from poet to entertainer was driven home to me while in my car about a month after the CLA reading, when *A Prairie Home Companion* came on the air, and the ever glib and oily-voiced Garrison Keillor announced that one of his guests tonight would be Billy Collins. Keillor and Collins are perfectly matched as poetry purveyors, tapping into the great hunger in the land for high-toned middlebrow mediocrity, the nonthreatening eloquence of self-help culture conscripting literature—often dark and bleak in its truths—as a vehicle to make people happy. Like the lofty sentimentality that Collins often mocks, the cut-rate sentiment of his famously "accessible" writing is a mannerism, a cheap trick worthy of the craftiest con artist. On Keillor's show, he proceeded to introduce, word for word as far as I could tell, several of the same poems he'd read in Sacramento, and strangely enough, they weren't as funny the second time. The studiedly neutral lilt of his voice, the practiced nonchalance, the deadpan timing, the easy patter with his smarmy host, all sounded to me like standup comedy—showbiz and nothing more.

Poetry (like the best comedy, for that matter) can be dangerous, thrilling, inspiring, disturbing, challenging, intellectually engaging, emotionally daring—it doesn't have to "traffic" in banality any more than it does in "obscurity or incomprehensibility." Collins has found his groove and is riding it as far as it will take him, but to compare him to a figure like Robert Frost, as *The Boston Globe* notably has, is an act of critical idiocy. Frost, for all his New England earthiness, is neither easy nor funny, and Collins, for all his Frosty downhomeness, has none of the knotty ambiguity of his predecessor, nor the grumpy toughness. The lightness of his touch, the apparent ease of his lines, is a strength that no comparison with Frost does anything to enhance. Collins is closer in spirit to some suburbanized combination of Frank O'Hara, William Carlos Williams, John Ashbery, Charles Bukowski and Ogden Nash—all investigators of the everyday whose use of the vernacular and ironic humor (though each in his own distinctive way) endear them to their admirers. Other distinguished contemporaries, like James Tate and Bill Knott and August Kleinzahler, deploy sharp comic wit in their work without compromising their inventive edge or writing according to a formula.

So why has Collins, a highly skilled poet but not an exceptional one in terms of imagination or originality, been turned into such a star? Surely he's worked at it, but ambition alone is not enough to generate such robust, Random House–worthy sales. Even before his 2001 appointment as US Poet Laureate he was a word-of-mouth sensation, and along with a handful of other brand-name bards has risen to assume a cultural role not just as a big-time writer but as the non-intimidating face of poetry, the poet who's just like you and me, a regular-guy poet, not one of those elitist, screwed-up traffickers in obscurity who deserve to remain obscure because they won't even stoop to meet the reader halfway. The American literary marketplace needs populists and publicists like Collins and Keillor because they prove that poetry can be nice, domesticated, friendly, easy—an uplifting form of lightweight entertainment.

Despite all this, or perhaps because of it, Billy Collins may be good for poetry if he demystifies it enough to encourage readers to go beyond their comfort zones and read some poets who may not be so cuddly. The positive side of the "trouble" with poetry, its pandemic contagion via the creative–writing–industrial complex, is that people, introduced to verse by the likes of Collins, may find their way not just to their own poems, or poetry as therapy, or MFA degrees, but to writers whose work they can return to over time and continue to find new pleasures, meanings, nuances, music, astonishment, unsettling ideas or devastating beauty—something more than analgesic amusement.

But Collins is right: the trouble with poetry is that it inspires the writing of more poetry. Where will it end? In this case, with my own "Sonnet to Billy Collins":

> Shall I compare thee to a happy dog
> that leaps to lick the reader's face with long
> wet tongue and smiling teeth and tail that wags
> ingratiatingly to win her love?
> Thou art more cute than even puppies are,
> and funnier than Maya Angelou,
> and better-selling than, say, Frank O'Hara,

and far more likable than Rilke, too.
Your poems make me feel so good about
myself and my ability to write
verses as good as yours, poems that might
make folks like me as much as I like you.
As long as jokes are told and minstrels play,
your lines will go on saying "Have a nice day."

2006

Points Beyond

Aleixandre the Great

1 A Poet's Journey

Vicente Aleixandre was born in Seville in 1898, spent most
of his childhood in the seacoast city of Málaga, and moved
to Madrid with his family at age eleven. As a young man he
studied business and law and read voraciously—mostly nine-
teenth-century novels—and at the age of eighteen discovered
poetry with the help of his good friend Dámaso Alonso (now
one of Spain's most eminent men of letters). The poet to whom
Alonso introduced him was the Nicaraguan Rubén Darío, pro-
genitor of modern poetry in Spanish. Soon after that, Aleixandre discovered Antonio Machado and Juan Ramón Jiménez,
two of Spain's reigning literary giants of the time, and began to
write verses of his own.

Aleixandre's first published poems appeared in José Ortega
y Gasset's *Revista del Occidente* in 1926. At this time there
were a number of other excellent young poets and artists
beginning to surface in the Spanish capital—among them Federico García Lorca, Rafael Alberti, Luis Buñuel, Jorge Guillén,
Salvador Dalí, Luis Cernuda, Pedro Salinas and Gerardo

Diego—whose imaginative energies were mutually magnetic, developing among themselves a lively network of friendships and common projects, social happenings and publications, which established a fertile subsoil for the flowering of the highly distinct artistic styles already starting to emerge. This group became known variously as the Generation of Friendship, Generation of the Republic, Generation of '25 or Generation of '27. Before the civil war began in 1936, the "generation" had stretched to embrace younger Spaniards like Manuel Altolaguirre and Miguel Hernández, as well as the South American Pablo Neruda, whose volcanic genius was very harmonious with the explosive powers of poets like Lorca and Aleixandre.

The latter, stricken with a severe kidney disorder about the same time he'd begun to write poetry, was forced to give up his career with a railroad company in the mid-1920s (both his father and Neruda's had been engineers) and spend the next several years in an intermittent state of semi-confinement. He lived then—as he does still—in his family home on the outskirts of Madrid, vacationing each summer in the Sierra de Guadarrama, and it was in the mountains that he began to write intensively. Alonso has interpreted this illness as some kind of divine intervention on behalf of poetry. In any case Aleixandre, despite his shaky health, became one of the prime forces in the Generation of '27, both as a poet of powerful originality and as a friend among friends. Most of the members of the "grupo poético" have recalled him in their writings as a warm and sympathetic person and a writer whose work was a revelation to them. His house—among other homes, cafés and taverns—became a central gathering place, where Lorca would play the piano and friendships were intensified through eating and drinking, conversation and the sharing of works in progress.

Ámbito, Aleixandre's first book (published in 1928), was a fairly conventional exercise in "pure poetry," heavily influenced by Jiménez and Machado. While the book demonstrated his technical skills and a distinctively refined sensibility, there was nothing particularly original about it. Then he read Freud (*The Interpretation of Dreams*) and Joyce (*Ulysses*), the combination of which was enough to blast away the constrictions still binding the range of impulses alive in the "sub-sky" of his imagination. In the next couple of years he wrote a series of extremely dense and wildly associative prose poems, first called *Evasión hacia el fondo* and later *Pasión de la tierra*. The book's composition is contemporaneous with Lorca's nightmarish *Poeta en Nueva York*, Alberti's *Sobre los ángeles*, and Neruda's *Residencia en la tierra*, exploring similar unconscious territory, dreamscape, grotesque humor, psychic terror and isolation, with a visceral kind of "surrealism" quite different from the highly self-conscious derangement of the French. Aleixandre himself had not even read the French poets then writing, but obviously there was something in the air (technological disillusionment? the Theory of Relativity? the cinema?) which led many writers to begin investigating the dimensions of the irrational.

As soon as the prose poems of *Pasión de la tierra* were behind him (still unpublished and unpublishable till five years later, and then only as a selection in a limited Mexican edition of which the author saw only a few copies) he went on with *Espadas como labios*, another book in a "surrealistic" style informed by a curious combination of eroticism and irony. This book contains some of Aleixandre's best satirical poems, poems designed in part to pierce the veil of social pretensions and reveal the sexual lava seething beneath the surface of polite society. There's a tone of defiance in these poems, a rebellious posturing and deliberate outrageousness not uncommon among poets just coming into their own. The paternal influence of Jiménez was fading fast, and Aleixandre was on the crest of his next big breakthrough, the poems of *La destrucción o el amor*.

It was this book—an eruption of extraordinary lyrical energy written in less than a year—which amazed his peers when it was passed around in manuscript toward the end of 1933. Despite the new ground broken in Lorca's recent work, and before that in Neruda's, no one was quite prepared for *La destrucción o el amor*, because here as nowhere before was a coherent yet wildly inventive erotic vision, a mystical immersion in the physical geography of love and its latent complement death. The stylistic mastery of these poems, the ungovernable unconscious dynamism wedded to a classical steadiness of expression in open form, the interplay of passion and elegant formality, established Aleixandre as a major voice and won him the National Prize for Literature.

Within a year or so after *La destrucción* was published in 1935, Franco's forces in exile invaded the Spanish Republic and the civil war had begun. In the first weeks García Lorca, everyone's favorite creative flame, was mysteriously executed by the local police in his native Granada. No one could believe it. Miguel Hernández, the Andalusian shepherd, went off to fight for the Republic and ended up in one of Franco's prisons, where he died still writing poems. Before long, most of the rest of the group left Spain for other parts of Europe, Latin

America and the United States. Aleixandre, still not entirely mobile, stayed at his family home and became an interior exile for the next eight years. During this time, when he could not publish and his name couldn't even be mentioned in print on account of his close association with many artists whom the Franquistas correctly regarded as their enemies, the poet would receive visits from many younger writers who had not personally known the members of the Generation of '27 but had been deeply affected by their work. The contact was mutually nourishing: Aleixandre, isolated from his former friends and associates, here had others with whom to share the creative adventure; and the younger poets, cut off from their revolutionary predecessors, had in Aleixandre a vital point of contact with that group. From this time on, Aleixandre was to become increasingly prominent in his poetic influence, eventually assuming the role of the resident *maestro* formerly played by Juan Ramón. More sociable and receptive than Jiménez, however, Aleixandre grew to be known as a remarkably generous "father figure" to the up-and-coming, who continued to visit him at home, the house itself developing into a natural point of reference for poets passing through Madrid.

In 1944, when finally permitted to publish again, Aleixandre astounded everyone with another huge book called *Sombra del paraíso*—a book which many consider to be his masterpiece—one of the most extravagant demonstrations ever of the fiery musicality of the Spanish language. The book is a luxuriously sensuous evocation of lost innocence—an elegiac celebration of his missing companions and a resurrection of a happy childhood by the sea—embodied in long melodious poems whose language is much more clear and direct than that of *La destrucción o el amor*, yet also more abstract and philosophical, set down in extended graceful lines so rich in edenic feeling that they present today's North American reader with an even more troublesome difficulty than that of his earlier, more "surrealistic" work. There is in these poems what seems at first glance to be a romantic overstatement of emotion, an adoption of traditional idyllic images and their ideas-by-association, which makes them in my opinion the most difficult of all his work to render in convincing English translation. Most of Aleixandre's work is very tough on a translator who cares about staying close to the original—it resists the transfer in a variety of ways, from tone and sound to imagery and syntax— but *Sombra del paraíso* is so utterly rooted in the resonances and rhythms of the poet's Castilian idiom, his technical virtuosity and depth of feeling, that there seem to be no sounds in English with which to create an analogous verbal experience. While I've worked with a great many poems from various periods in his *obra*, and feel by virtue of intuition and familiarity to have a fairly good grasp of how to render the poet's voice, *Sombra del paraíso* remains an enigma to me as a translator. (This is ironic because to Spanish readers at the time, *Sombra del paraíso* was Aleixandre's most accessible work to date, eloquently manifesting his idea that "poetry is communication.")

From the mid-1940s on, Aleixandre continued to develop his powers as one of the leading poets of the age, publishing big collections in 1954 (*Historia del corazón*) and 1962 (*En un vasto dominio*) which further displayed the great range of his voices, exploring themes of love, the city, memory and the metaphysics of human anatomy. In 1966 he finished *Poemas de la consumación*, poems with the radiant serenity of old age, and in 1973 *Diálagos del conocimiento*, a collection in which he abandons the lyric forms of which he is a master for that of the dramatic dialogue. The directness and clarity of the later poems is even more simply communicative—still very sensual but aphoristic, philosophically serene, accepting, pervaded by a deeply religious faith in the creation. Beyond the individual works of genius scattered throughout his career, it is the immense scope of his poetry that most impresses me—his ability to inhabit so many different voices and attitudes, each arising naturally out of the other. The "pure" poet gives way to the miner of the psychic underground whose writings are expressive but scarcely comprehensible; the dream-excavator yields to the terrorizer of the bourgeoisie (a parallel to Buñuel's work in the cinema), and the anguished satirist evolves in turn into the passionate lyric poet singing of the cosmic joys and hazards of erotic love. Then there emerges the symphonic re-creation of a mythic childhood—a paradise inside the mind, whose shadow is poetry—and later the luminous poems of personal love, a calm identification with the rest of humanity (with the lingering gift of satire for dismantling pretensions), the acceptance of the completion that comes with death, delicious harvest of a long life resonating in the memory.

Before he was awarded the Nobel Prize, Aleixandre remained virtually unheard-of in this country. To people familiar with modern poetry his name was known, but few had any experience of his work. Now there is bound to be more attention paid to his writings here, and probably an edition of selected poems issued by some New York publisher hoping to cash in on the Nobel aftershocks. For the sake of those unable to read the original Spanish we can only hope that the translations made widely available be faithful to the meaning, the tone, the feeling and the music of Aleixandre's poems, giving the reader as vivid a sense as possible of "what it would be like" to read the Castilian. That has been my intention as a translator.

1977

2 *Nobel Confidential*

Remember Vicente Aleixandre?

Well, how about Jaroslav Seifert?

Or Harry Martinson?

Or Saint-John Perse, perhaps?

Surely you haven't already forgotten Wislawa Szymborska?

Szymborska, the Polish poet, was last year's Nobel laureate in literature. Seifert (Czech, 1984), Martinson (Swedish, 1974) and Perse (French, 1960) are a few of the other non-Anglophone Nobel poets of the last forty years. Aleixandre, a Spaniard and my favorite among these for personal reasons, received the prize twenty years ago—coincidentally the 50th anniversary of Spain's stellar Generation of 1927. With the long-drawn-out death of dictator Francisco Franco the previous year, the Swedish Academy evidently felt it was time to give Spain the nod and chose Aleixandre, that country's seventy-nine-year-old resident master, to receive the world's loftiest literary honor.

After their fifteen minutes of Nobelized fame, many great foreign writers of international renown tend to fade from our short-term memories. Poets, laureled or unsung, local or exotic, at best aren't likely to be noticed much in this country. With notable exceptions like Allen Ginsberg (a political activist and tireless self-promoter who made himself unignorable) and Pablo Neruda (Nobel 1971, who hit it big with the US public only when played by Philippe Noiret in the 1995 movie *Il Postino*), even the most distinguished bards routinely toil in relative obscurity for a fairly limited audience. For those who write in languages other than English, the Nobel rarely changes their marginal status in the popular imagination.

At the time Aleixandre won the prize there were just two small editions of his poetry in print in American translation. Two years later, in 1979, Harper & Row brought out Lewis Hyde's edition of Aleixandre's selected poems, *A Longing for the Light*. Left to go out of print by Harper & Row, the book was picked up in 1985 and reprinted in paperback by Copper Canyon Press, the independent poetry publisher in Port Townsend, Washington. UC Press, around 1992, no doubt with good intentions, brought out a painfully tone-deaf translation of one of Aleixandre's most beautiful books, *Shadow of Paradise*. But *A Longing for the Light*, while representing only a fragment of his work, remains the only readable collection of Aleixandre's poetry available in a US edition. (Full disclosure: I have a few translations in that book.)

A semi-invalid for most of his adult life due to tuberculosis and the removal of one kidney, Aleixandre died in 1984 at the age of eighty-six, having outlived most of his healthier contemporaries. He had seen the best minds of his generation destroyed or exiled by a bloody civil war and a forty-year fascist dictatorship, and managed to record the grief of those years as well as a generously compassionate wisdom in a series of lyric and elegiac books that run to some two thousand pages of poetry and prose. In his most luminous writing—in books like *Sombra del paraíso*, *Historia del corazón* and *En un vasto dominio*—there is an openheartedness and melodic richness seldom encountered in English-language verse and even more rarely realized in translation.

Apart from the inherent limits of the market, undoubtedly one reason for the shortage of Aleixandre's (and other foreign Nobel winners') works in English is the difficulty his writing presents for translators. I know this because in 1977 my version of his 1933 book *Destruction or Love* was one of the two slim volumes of his verse available in this country. The other was *Twenty Poems of Vicente Aleixandre*, translated by Lewis Hyde and issued by Robert Bly's The Seventies Press. It was Bly who telephoned, that sunny October morning twenty years ago, to give me the good news and to ask a few questions about the old man, whom I'd seen in Madrid the previous year. Bly was doing an essay for *The New York Times Book Review*, which, when it appeared a couple of weeks later, ensured that the thousand copies of my book (printed by Berkeley's Wesley Tanner and published by Green Horse Press in Santa Cruz) would sell out in short order and give me a glint of glory by association.

With or without that stroke of luck I'd still be grateful to the Spanish poet for the unofficial apprenticeship he provided me. Translating anyone is an act of impersonation, but to bring alive in a new language the work of a master means you must stretch your voice beyond the limits of its usual range, sharpen your technical skills and expand your imagination. Beyond the radiance of his artistry, Aleixandre's graciousness and encouragement were invaluable to me, not only in the project we did together but in all my subsequent efforts as a writer.

I'd met him through a series of chance encounters in Madrid in 1973, taken to his house in the city's outskirts by little-magazine editor Gonzalo Armero, who informed me that a visit to Aleixandre at home was an essential pilgrimage for any young poet in Spain. I didn't know it then, but the house was legendary, the same one where a constellation of creative talent had often gathered in the late 1920s and early 1930s to cultivate poetic friendships. Federico García Lorca, Rafael Alberti, Jorge Guillén, Luis Cernuda, Dámaso Alonso, Pedro Salinas, Luis Buñuel, Salvador Dalí and even the South American Neruda (who served as Chilean consul in pre–civil war Spain) had been among the young geniuses erupting like some collective volcano in and around the capital at the time.

When the 1936 civil war scattered—or, in Lorca's case, murdered—most of these artists, Aleixandre, due to his fragile health, remained at his family home, a kind of internal exile, officially silenced for years on account of his loyalty to the Republic that Franco had overthrown. Eventually he would assume the role of chief living link between his tragic generation and those that followed. Over the years he became a godfather figure to younger Spanish poets, whom he encouraged tirelessly through frequent personal meetings and daily postal correspondence.

As I was to learn in that first and succeeding visits, one made an appointment by phone with the maestro and arrived precisely on time. Aleixandre was an Old World gentleman of meticulous habits and fixed routines, impeccably dressed that summer afternoon in his standard domestic attire of slacks and necktie and cardigan sweater, his pinkish bald head gleaming and blue eyes blazing with an icy-bright color I've never seen anywhere else. Fastidiously ensconced in the dimness of his library, its bookcases heavy with history, Don Vicente (as Gonzalo addressed him, in the traditional manner) was formal in a way but delightfully animated, congenially engaging me in conversation about my work. Told of my budding interest in translation, by the end of the visit he was urging me to translate his favorite among his own books, *La destrucción o el amor*, which had won him the Premio Nacional de Literatura forty years earlier but had never been done in English.

It was a daunting proposal for a twenty-six-year-old poet, but as I had synchronistically purchased a copy of that book a few days earlier—without even knowing whether the author was still alive, let alone that I was about to meet him—I told him I'd take it home and write to him once I had a chance to study the poems. Like other poets of the Generation of '27, Aleixandre had been immersed in Europe's intellectual and artistic currents of that decade—Freud's unearthing of the unconscious, Joyce's stream-of-consciousness technique, early experiments in film (discontinuous cutting and unexpected juxtapositions, most radically in Buñuel and Dalí's *Un chien andalou*), surrealism in its less doctrinaire and more intuitive manifestations than André Breton's Parisian manifestos demanded. *Destruction or Love* had evolved in part from these sources as well as out of the densely oneiric prose poems of the author's earlier book *Pasión de la tierra*; *La destrucción*, he told me, was written as he recovered from his life-changing illness, "in an irruption of health and vital appetite."

Reading the lavishly surreal erotic lyrics of *La destrucción o el amor*, tentatively feeling my way through their jungle of visionary imagery and long-lined syntax, registering the emotional turbulence of their sensuality combined with a certain classical elegance of rhetoric, I understood why they had remained untranslated: they were untranslatable. But after some false starts and the exchange of a few letters with the poet—whose only real guidance was to point me to the poems he thought most important—I somehow found a way in and, within a couple of years, was able to finish twenty-two translations sound enough to represent a version of the original, much longer book.

In 1976, with the Green Horse edition at the printer, I returned to Madrid with my romantic companion and we arranged another visit with Don Vicente. We showed up at five o'clock sharp, as instructed, and he seemed pleased to see us. I had with me a copy of the final manuscript, and he was especially interested in my Translator's Preface; I had referred to Neruda as an influence on his generation of Spanish poets, but Aleixandre corrected me: It was not a matter of influence, it was friendship. The greatest influence on his generation had been Luis de Góngora, the sixteenth-century Spanish poet whose baroque style permeated many of their early works. Partly in reaction against the "pure poetry" of regnant master Juan Ramón Jiménez (Nobel 1956), the younger Spaniards found in Góngora a classic if neglected example of marvelously *impure* poetry.

But the thing he said to us that day that most vividly stayed with me had nothing directly to do with literature. He had been reminiscing about the days when García Lorca would play the piano here in this house and other young friends would congregate to socialize. These memories were wonderful, he wistfully admitted, but they were all he had left of his lost companions and those intoxicating times. He fixed his seventy-eight-year-old fiery blue eyes on us—both under thirty—and said, with almost frightening intensity, *Ustedes tienen la juventud*, as if that were the most important thing in the world: You have your youth—you're young! This declaration was strangely moving then, but in a way I'm only now, at fifty, beginning to understand.

The following year came his Nobel Prize, and Aleixandre's name, already revered in literary Spain, was broadcast around the globe, suddenly unsettling his tranquil routine. His professional correspondence, which he had maintained entirely himself in his graceful if increasingly shaky fountain-pen script, was taken over by the formidable Carmen Balcells, queen of Spanish literary agents, who contacted me for a complete accounting of my Aleixandre publications and instructed me that all future permissions would have to come through her. The stakes had been definitively raised.

The poet had written me an enthusiastic letter in response to our published book, and I stayed in touch with him as best I could until, in the summer of 1978, I again arranged to see him at home in Madrid.

When he opened the door for me that afternoon he looked aged beyond the two years since I'd seen him last. He showed a mixture of boyish pride and geezerly annoyance in having bagged the Nobel. *Es un reclám*, he said to me, half gloating, half disgusted: It's a clamorous demand, a resounding acclaim—and a calamitous disruption of one's life.

Japanese reporters, Italian photographers, German publishers, and television crews from all over Europe had descended on his quiet neighborhood—no doubt disturbing the nuns at the convent next door—without observing the protocol of calling for an appointment. Demands for interviews were ceaseless, and the nightmare of celebrity went on for weeks. The stress had given him an excruciating attack of shingles, and he said he'd thought the ordeal would finish him off. For all the satisfaction he took in the honor and recognition and money bestowed by the Nobel committee, the prize had been, for him personally, *un catástrofe*.

He was, he told me, just beginning to recover and had been receiving few visitors lately, but since I'd come all the way from California in this case he'd made an exception. He apologized for his lingering depression, but as we talked he grew perkier, and by the time our brief visit was over he was thanking me for having cheered him up. We embraced at the front door as the sun was going down, and as I left he gave me a long warm goodbye look through those bright blue unforgettable eyes.

Then, for the last few years of his life, as far as most of the world was concerned, slowly, peacefully, Vicente Aleixandre faded back into the merciful twilight of obscurity.

1997

Dr. Joy:
Fernando Alegría

A few months after the September 11, 1973, coup in Chile and the death of Salvador Allende, followed less than two weeks later by Pablo Neruda's death amid the bloody takeover of the country by General Augusto Pinochet's military dictatorship, Chilean writer, professor and diplomat Fernando Alegría came to UC Santa Cruz to read his poetry. The reading was arranged by George Hitchcock, who was teaching there at the time and had published under his Kayak imprint Alegría's long surrealist satirical political poem *Instructions for Undressing the Human Race.* Alegría, later the chairman of the Department of Spanish and Portuguese at Stanford, had been President Allende's cultural attaché for the Chilean Embassy in Washington and had spent much of those last three years promoting goodwill for the socialist government in Santiago. Now deeply involved with the Chilean intelligentsia in exile, he never broke stride in his writing, continuing to turn out a steady stream of fiction, poetry, essays and criticism, editing anthologies and authoring textbooks while tending to his academic duties and maintaining his political engagement.

That night in Santa Cruz in 1974 marked the start of a friendship whose reverberations I'm still feeling. I was just beginning to publish as a translator, and Fernando, recognizing what I might have to offer his own literary agenda, wasted no time in cajoling me into his camp. I sent him a broadside Green Horse Press had done of my version of Vicente Aleixandre's "I Am Destiny" and Fernando immediately wrote back thanking me, praising the translation and inviting me to come to his home soon for a swim and dinner. And so began his cagey seduction of me and my fledgling talent, plying me with Chilean wine and meals cooked by his wife, Carmen—whose own tough-minded intelligence, wit and kindness I'd grow to love in the coming years—enticing me and my nubile companion Hollis into his backyard sauna, chasing the naked Hollis around the pool much to our confused amusement, and generally charming the pants off both of us.

Like Fernando Rey in Buñuel's *That Obscure Object of Desire,* Fernando A. was drawn to youthful beauty; the flirtatious gentleman was also serious, funny, political, playful, earnest, ironic, warmly affectionate, a bon vivant, an activist, a raconteur, an entrepreneur—traits not ordinarily found combined so richly in a single personality. When we traveled together to readings or conferences over the next dozen years or so, I saw how this gourmet blend of qualities inevitably earned the fondness and admiration of people we met, and witnessed the vast network of his friendships with writers from all over the Americas. One of Fernando's claims to fame was his widely taught history of the Latin American novel, whose expanded second edition was issued amid "El Boom" of the 1960s. Mention the name of virtually any famous contemporary Spanish-language writer and Fernando would say, "He's a good friend of mine," and launch into an anecdote about some colorful incident—Neruda worried at a post-reading party in Berkeley that Allen Ginsberg would cause a scandal by taking off his clothes, Borges lapping milk from a saucer like a housecat, Vargas Llosa's movie-star persona deployed to full effect at some PEN event—genial and sometimes mildly malicious gossip about the greats of current literature. When Juan Rulfo of Mexico or Ernesto Cardenal of Nicaragua or the Argentine-Parisian Julio Cortázar came to the Bay Area, Fernando would inevitably throw a low-key but lively party for the guest that included abundant food and drink and multilingual conversation.

When the mullahs of Iran put a million-dollar bounty on the head of Salman Rushdie for his supposedly blasphemous *Satanic Verses* and the book's sales went through the roof, Fernando observed that Rushdie, in hiding, was now so rich that "He should offer two million to anyone who *doesn't* kill him." During the Central American civil wars of the seventies and eighties when he was constant in his support of Marxist insurgencies against right-wing CIA-backed regimes and one of his daughters expressed her desire for her young son to grow up to be part of the revolution, Fernando dismissed this idea with the opinion that he should instead be a banker. He advised me more than once never to accept less than top dollar when commissioned to do translations but somehow always managed in our own collaborations to get me to work for a token fee from the publisher, if not for free. These kinds of ironies made him somehow all the more endearing and entertaining to be around, his wit and his contradictions forever poised to surprise.

The 1976 car bomb assassination of his friend Orlando

Letelier, Allende's ambassador to the US and leader of the Chilean exile community during the Pinochet regime, made Fernando fear for his own safety. He had been in Chile at the time of the coup and was lucky to have escaped unscathed. If Pinochet's secret police could murder Letelier in the middle of Washington, how hard would it be to ambush him on the Stanford campus? During the late seventies he was much more cautious about opening his door to unexpected guests, more suspicious of strange men who might be following him, worried about what the CIA might be doing to monitor his contacts. And yet he never let up, either at his desk or in his social and political life, turning out book after book for his Mexican and South American and Spanish publishers, supporting cultural causes, speaking in public, traveling, eating and drinking and schmoozing, making new friends and cultivating old ones.

Fernando had gotten his PhD in English literature at Berkeley in 1947 and taught there through most of the fifties and sixties. His 1970 novel *Amerika Amerikka Amerikkka* (published later in my translation as *The Funhouse*) chronicles the surreal and frightening and darkly uproarious misadventures of a Latin American immigrant in a community of similarly displaced persons in a setting that feels much like Berkeley in the sixties, replete with rampant sex and promiscuous substance abuse and a sense of hallucinatory disorientation in a Boschian urban landscape of outrageous excess. The novel catches the freaky spirit of its time and place in a way that only a non-native could have experienced it. He told me he'd moved across the Bay for the warmer, sunnier climate, but I suspect the prestige and the money were better too, and Stanford a less tumultuous community.

Another project we worked on together was the anthology *Chilean Writers in Exile*, the centerpiece of which was his creepy novella *Coral de Guerra (War Chorale)*, a post-coup tale of horror in the form of a three-way dialogue between a disappeared and tortured leftist activist, her military captor and her husband, who is seeking information about her fate. The psychological penetration and formal and stylistic strangeness of *War Chorale* led one reviewer to compare it to Joyce and Faulkner. "Not bad," Fernando remarked to me, pleased to be accorded in the United States even a fraction of the respect routinely earned by his books in Latin America. Though he was for many years the most distinguished Latin American writer in the Bay Area and well beyond, he never quite enjoyed the stardom of some of his peers, so any acknowledgment of his creative powers in his adopted land meant a lot to him.

Changing Centuries, his selected poems in English, displays the range of his lyric voices, from surrealist jokester to tender sonneteering grandfather to erotic lover to inflammatory polemicist. His English was a lot more fluent than my Spanish, but in consulting on my versions of his poems he never tried to micromanage the language. Knowing I'd do my best to get the meaning right, his standing instruction was "Just make it sound good." He even occasionally encouraged me to keep mistakes if they seemed to him an improvement on the original.

His other books in English range from his popular comic novel *Caballo de Copas (My Horse Gonzalez)*, a racetrack tale based in part on his own experience as a horse owner, to the grim historical narratives *El Paso de los Gansos* (literally *The Goose Step* or *Goosesteppers*, published in the US as *The Chilean Spring*) and *Allende*. I asked Fernando how he managed to be so prolific while maintaining his teaching and administrative schedule at Stanford, his active social and political life and even his frequent rounds of golf or trips to the track. Perhaps it had something to do with his daily Royal Canadian Mountie exercise routine, or the regular sauna and swim, but he told me that the trick was to get up by 6:00 a.m. and work until about 11:00, leaving the rest of the day free for other activities, including a siesta after lunch.

Alegría means *joy* in Spanish. When we would occasionally go out to dinner at his favorite Chinese restaurant in Palo Alto, he'd make the reservation under "Dr. Joy," and when the maitre d' would greet him by that name we'd all have a good laugh. His preferred bourbon was Maker's Mark, in the fat bottle with the red wax seal. He often carried a little silver flask in his coat pocket when we'd go to the city for readings or other literary or political festivities. He called me "Estephen" and introduced me to many people who would greatly expand my professional relations as a writer and translator, and extend the web of my friendships—his former students Francisco Alarcón and Juan Felipe Herrera, Julio Cortázar and his wife Carol Dunlop, Ariel Dorfman, even Joan Baez, with whom we appeared at some rally or other.

We went to Mexico City together in 1982 for the Dialogue of the Americas, a cross-cultural conference held mainly at the Museum of Anthropology, where I met and fell in love with a gorgeous young Mexican Leninist and where Fernando wrote and read to the delegates an untranslatable poem called "Diálogo de los Sordos" ("Dialogue of the Deaf"), provoking some of the biggest laughs of the meeting. A couple of years later I was sent to Cuba for a smaller, follow-up gathering, where I drank mojitos with the minister of culture and other leftist literati, and smoked contraband on the beach one night with some young black men who complained in low tones that, sure, they had free health care and education, "But we don't have freedom!" I was Fernando's emissary on this trip, and it broadened and complicated my sense of Cuban reality. How could I not be grateful for such experience?

When I became more deeply engaged in journalism in Santa Cruz, as a columnist and feature writer, and eventually grew insane enough to start my own weekly newspaper, *The Sun*, Fernando knew he was losing my steady services as a translator but never stopped encouraging my efforts to infiltrate a non-literary medium with the subversive imagination of a poet. He complimented me on my personal essays by comparing them to those of Charles Lamb, the English Romantic I'd scarcely read in the course of getting my master's. His casual familiarity with the British tradition, which I had largely rejected in my post–graduate-school rebellion against most things old and white, only increased my respect for the depth and breadth of his learning. Our friendship continued, but our get-togethers came at longer intervals.

The last time I saw him was in 1998 when my version of Cortázar's selected poems came out and I asked if he would introduce me at a reading in Palo Alto. Carmen, who had made his writing life possible by keeping the household together after abandoning her own career in medicine, had died a few years earlier, and Fernando never recovered from her loss. The welcoming house adjacent to Stanford where we had enjoyed so many festive lunches and dinners and congenial gatherings felt cold and spookily desolate, and he was beginning to show the early signs of Alzheimer's, which was to cloud the final years of his life. His introduction of my reading that night at Printers Inc. went on for a rambling twenty minutes or so with stories about Borges and García Márquez and whatever other associations came into his head until I had to stage-whisper from the front row, "Hey, Fernando, don't forget to introduce me!" He paused, went on with his monologue a little longer, and finally presented me to the audience. At the back of the room was an Argentinian woman who objected to my California Spanish when I read one of Cortázar's poems in the original. I looked at Fernando in the front row and asked him, "How come nobody gives you a hard time about your accent?" As if to prove his wits were still sharp, he replied deadpan in his Chilean English, "I don't have an accent."

When his daughter Carmen Delia called me in early November to say that he'd died a few days before, surrounded by his family in the nursing home where he'd spent his last few years, I wasn't really surprised, as I knew he'd been ill for a long time. He was eighty-seven and had lived a life of extraordinary richness and accomplishment. What hurt was that I was in Montreal at a translation conference—fittingly enough, since he had done so much to lead me further and deeper into that practice—and was unable to attend the funeral. I'm told that his children and grandchildren and many of his wide array of friends and former students and colleagues gave him a send-off worthy of his personage, concluding with a song by Rafael Manriquez, the forceful invocation by a voice in the crowd, *"Compañero Fernando Alegría!"* and the collective response, *"Presente!"*

2006

Ernesto Cardenal
in San Francisco

---

1 Politics at the Fine Arts

Ernesto Cardenal's arrival in San Francisco was anticipated
with great agitation in the political and literary communities.
Through his poetry Nicaragua's Minister of Culture has distinguished himself for many years as one of Latin America's
leading writers. As a priest and political activist, and now as
a member of the government, he has been and continues to
be a significant presence in the revolution. Although Cardenal has claimed that he'd like to return to his little community
of Solentiname on Lake Nicaragua and resume his work as a
poet and priest—instead of being an administrator, diplomat
and some kind of spiritual engineer for the Sandinistas—he's
clearly committed to his current job as long as his country's
revolutionary experiment is threatened by the likes of Ronald
Reagan.

Reagan's aggressions against the people of Central America
have begun to bring out the activist in North American artists
and intellectuals who realize their "personal" lives may not
be livable without their also working on the public front. For

many such people Cardenal is a beacon, an example of poetry's social role and of spiritual values actively wedded to ethics. Much of his best work happens off the page.

Of course he's been remarkable on paper too, turning out major poems since the mid-1960s. "Apocalypse," "Zero Hour," "Oracle over Managua" and *Homage to the American Indians* are among his many texts certain to increase in meaning and power with time. Like Neruda in his epic *Canto General*— although stylistically more like Pound and Ginsberg, whom he acknowledges as major influences—Cardenal grounds his writing in historical sources, reconstructing or documenting on-the-spot from a personal perspective events whose significance is shared by a large collective. Some twenty years before the bomb became a big deal for most North American poets (the Beats were a notable exception to the silence of the respectable literati on this issue), Cardenal's "Apocalypse" ripped the lid off nuclear holocaust as an imaginable subject for a poem. His poems on Nicaraguan history have a journalistic quickness and eyewitness immediacy even when he's writing about the past. The vividness and energy of his style may have something to do with the intensity of faith he brings to his work of building a new culture.

In Nicaragua, since the Sandinista triumph of 1979, culture is not a costly imported decoration for the ruling class to hang on its walls and admire with a faint estheticism, it is a presence in people's lives: the arts are flourishing in the new Nicaragua at a popular level, as something to *do* in workshops, at cultural festivals, at home and in the street. Cardenal's vision has been instrumental in generating an indigenous concept and process of cultural life in his country. A group of Bay Area artists and media people visited Nicaragua last summer and were moved by what they found there to form an organization called Friends of Nicaraguan Culture. It was this group that brought Cardenal to San Francisco's Palace of Fine Arts as the featured guest at its inaugural event, "Breaking the Blockade of Ideas."

The title of the program was particularly apt, as just a day or two earlier Nicaragua's Interior Minister Tomás Borge was denied a visa to visit the United States. Rumor was that Reagan himself had decided to ban Borge because he might use his speaking tour for "propaganda" purposes. The denial of Borge's visa was ingeniously timed to coincide with that of Salvadoran maniac Roberto D'Aubuisson, to give some illusion of "balance" between the Sandinista leader and the Salvadoran strongman commonly acknowledged as an enthusiastic backer of right-wing death squads. The Sandinistas' nonviolent rehabilitation of former Somoza guardsmen—the death penalty was one of the first things abolished after the victory—is an interesting contrast to the barbaric state of affairs in El Salvador. In any case, Borge was considered too dangerous to be let loose in this country without his free speech getting out of hand. If people are allowed to meet and speak with the alleged "threat to our national security," they may begin to realize he's no threat.

Borge was quoted lately as saying that it would take more than the Marines to overthrow a government with as much popular support as that of the Sandinistas, who have distributed arms to virtually the entire population. Imagine, suggested Borge, what would happen if Pinochet were to do that in Chile. The Nicaraguan people are determined to defend their revolution; their commitment is absolute and, despite the sabotage and terrorism of CIA-backed *contras* based in Honduras and Costa Rica, morale inside the country remains high. In order to defeat such a people, according to Borge, US troops would need the assistance of "Superman, Spiderman and Batman."

The Sandinistas believe that if they can communicate directly with the North American people, such human contact can help build a barricade against violent intervention. An open invitation has been extended to North Americans—artists, intellectuals, teachers, church people, trade unionists, doctors, engineers—to come to Nicaragua and see firsthand what is happening there. The haze of Reaganoid rhetoric which attempts to paint the Sandinistas as dangerous communists doing the bidding of the Soviet demon is a lie which can be exposed by people willing to encounter what's really going on and conveying their impressions back home. Friends of Nicaraguan Culture was organized to facilitate such ongoing contact.

If Reagan thought that Tomás Borge was a dangerous customer to have on our soil, it's anybody's guess how Cardenal got cleared. The president must have figured that since Cardenal is just a priest and poet, he must be fairly harmless. In fact, he was detained coming through customs, his bag was searched and his books inspected despite his diplomatic credentials. Cardenal said the scene reminded him of entering Nicaragua under Somoza.

The Palace of Fine Arts was sold out in advance and hundreds were turned away at the door the evening of December 2. When the crowd of over a thousand people finally packed itself into their seats and standing-room spots in the hall after extended milling in the cavernous lobby amidst poster exhibits and literature tables and refreshments and familiar faces from the poetry-and-activism networks of Northern California—not to mention the pamphlets and magazines being passed around free, all the urgent festivity of politics mixed with art—they were warmed up for the main event by San Francisco literary heroes Alice Walker and Michael McClure reading from their works; Berkeley mayor Gus Newport declaring the importance of solidarity with movements for independence among our hemispheric neighbors; actor David Clennon discussing what it was like to play the US consul in the movie *Missing*; and emcee Ronnie Davis, founder of the San Francisco Mime Troupe.

It was, however, Cardenal whom the people had come to see. The poet was introduced to a standing ovation which spontaneously turned to a chant of NO PASARÁN, they won't get through. Cardenal is a little man in his late fifties, with a silver-white beard and shaggy hair, baggy blue jeans, tan jacket, big glasses and a black beret. He has a powerful resonant voice which commands attention. He began with the first poem he wrote on the revolutionary triumph, a poem called "Lights," about flying over the country with other members of the new governing junta on the eve of victory, drawing connections between the lights of the stars and the lights of the liberated cities, connections between the sun, the moon and human bodies, a poem both mystical and journalistic.

English versions were read by Roberto Vargas, poet and cultural attaché with the Nicaraguan Embassy in Washington, and Cardenal followed with the originals in booming oratorical tones. He read about ten poems written since the triumph, and one from the era of Somoza, "The Arrival," about being detained at the Managua airport on returning from a trip abroad. In the eyes of the customs clerk the poet sees a confirmation of his dream of a new Nicaragua. The other poems testified to the challenge of making the dream reality. Cardenal's commitment to his changing country was conveyed with great enthusiasm, his lines rolling forth in incantatory waves. Apart from brief introductory remarks, he made no speeches, had no extraneous statements, he simply let his poetry do the talking.

The texts he read were plain as daylight, vividly straightforward, lovingly focused on the sights and sounds and smells of his native surroundings, full of colors and place names and specific historical references. There's also an inspired sense of the new society, of history in the making, of exhilaration at participating in a great experiment. The "poetic newspapers" he invokes in one of his poems are just the flip side of the visionary lyrics and documentary narratives in which he sets down current events. The future is alive in Cardenal's writing because he keeps in mind the ideal community which he and his *compañeros* are working to create.

The clarity of what he had to say combined with the political context of his appearance at this highly partisan gathering charged every poem with an electrifying immediacy. The audience raved its gratitude and approval. It was a reading of the highest order, and not a bad political rally either.

2 *Lunch with Ernesto*

Next day at noon there was a lunch in North Beach at the New Pisa, a legendary family-style Italian restaurant with

pictures of baseball players all over the walls. Lawrence Ferlinghetti played the role of host while Ronnie Davis directed
traffic with regard to who got close to the guest of honor. A
couple of dozen writers, poets, reporters and other entourage
of Cardenal's visit to the city enjoyed a meaty meal, after which
several of us clustered informally around the guest for further
conversation. Participants in this collective interview included
Ferlinghetti, poet Eugene Ruggles, writer and radio journalist
Larry Bensky, composer Charles Amirkhanian, Chicano poet
and cultural activist Francisco Alarcón, and myself. What follows is a slightly edited transcript of our discussion, which
began with someone asking which North American poets are
read in Nicaragua and Cardenal responding that Whitman,
Williams, Sandburg, Frost, Rukeyser and especially Pound are
all important presences for him and other Nicaraguan poets.
Ruggles asked about the current influence of Neruda.

Cardenal: For us in Spanish, Neruda is not new. For instance,
Muriel Rukeyser or Sandburg for you, it is not something new;
for us, it is. Or Kenneth Fearing. I don't know if Kenneth Fearing is read now in the United States; for us, it is something
very new.

Bensky: Ernesto, when people admire Ezra Pound, what do
you say to them about his politics and his life? How do you
explain that somebody with such magnificent technical abili-
ties took the points of view that he did?

Cardenal: You don't find his politics in his poetry, not even
in *The Cantos*. I mean his admiration for Mussolini, there were
only a few quotations about that. He was not a fascist, because
he was not defending the fascist methods. He was an admirer
of Mussolini, and that was a mistake, but he didn't admire the

fascist methods and he was always writing against capitalism—against usury, that is, capitalism. I think he is a Marxist poet. I think his poetry is Marxist, because the theme of his poetry is economic.

Bensky: Do you think Ezra Pound was a Marxist poet, Lawrence?

Ferlinghetti: No, he was a Confucianist and an elitist.

Ruggles: I think American poetry should forget about Ezra Pound. He was anti-Semitic and he was bordering on fascism.

Cardenal: Hm?

Ruggles: He didn't like Jewish people.

Cardenal: Some of his best friends were Jews. When he attacked Jews, he was attacking capitalism, not a race.

Ferlinghetti: What Pound had in mind were the big Jewish financiers who were running American finance.

Ruggles: Most Jewish people aren't rich. Most of them don't have much money at all. And they have a lot of dead ancestors from persecution throughout the ages.

Cardenal: Do you know that I am a Jew?

Ferlinghetti: Sephardic?

Cardenal: No. From Germany. From Königsberg, the city of Kant. My great-grandfather came from that city, with the name of Teufel, and he changed his name to Martínez—my second name is Martinez, but that is because he changed the name—but I should have been called Cardenal Teufel. That means "devil" in German. It is a Jewish name. That is my second last name.

Ferlinghetti: Your great-grandfather was a Jewish financier?

Cardenal: He went to Nicaragua because he wanted to go to California for the Gold Rush, and he became involved with the politics of Nicaragua and was imprisoned and condemned to death; and he asked to be baptized, and he asked the president of Nicaragua to be his godfather (laughs) and the president was Tomás Martínez, and after the baptism he would make him free (laughs), so he was not shot, and in gratitude he changed his name for the name of the president, and that is why my family has that name, Martínez. Cardenal is my mother's last name.

Alarcón: Nicaragua has been very important in terms of poetry in Latin America—Rubén Darío and *modernismo* and yourself with the school of *vitalismo* and all that—what do you see as the new trends in Nicaraguan poetry?

Cardenal: We have two. One is what I will call abstract poetry, and the other one concrete poetry. The abstract poetry is without any personal name, any specific thing of reality, just some kind of surrealism, I would say, or non-realist poetry. And the other one is a poetry that could talk about Somoza or Fidel Castro or Angola or Grenada or Nicaragua or Venezuela or many things, and places and streets and cities and rivers and mountains and first names.

Kessler: Like yours.

Cardenal: Or like the poetry of Ezra Pound and Ferlinghetti and Ginsberg, with anecdotes and jokes and many things. So we have two currents, and they are in conflict.

Alarcón: You don't have a solution between the two?

Cardenal: Some poets have both of them.

Kessler: And is there a dialog between the currents?

Cardenal (laughing): It is difficult to have a dialog because on one side they say, "That is not poetry, that is prose, that is a pamphlet for political purposes," and the other side says, "That is not revolutionary poetry, that poetry is not Nicaraguan poetry, that poetry is nonsense."

Kessler: But is it possible for the "abstract" writers to publish in Nicaragua now? Is there a circulation of both kinds of poetry?

Cardenal: I would say the abstract poets are more in power than the other ones (laughs) because they have the literary supplement of the Sandinista newspaper and they have a lot of criticism against the other poetry.

Kessler: So there must be some dialogue then, if they're criticizing each other in public.

Cardenal: Polemic, more than dialogue.

Alarcón: What about the new workshops, the literary workshops all over Nicaragua?

Cardenal: They belong to the realist poetry, or concrete poetry, with great influence of North American poetry; and the other side says, "That is not good poetry, that is a pamphlet, that is socialist realism" (laughs). That is a very bad insult, to be called "socialist realism"!

Ruggles: Ernesto, what do you think is going to happen in El Salvador in the next six months?

Cardenal: The guerrillas are stronger and stronger every day. The Salvadoran army is going to be defeated at any time. They need more and more help from the United States, otherwise they would be defeated overnight. And that is our problem, because we think that Reagan will not permit that defeat and he will intervene in Central America—in Salvador and Nicaragua.

Alarcón: Many people say that poetry and art which is

committed to revolution or national liberation is easier to write when the writers are out of power than when they are in power. Do you think this changes when art and literature are in power? When the revolution has been victorious, is it more difficult to write?

Cardenal: No. We have not seen that in Nicaragua. We have very good poetry now, since the triumph of the revolution: there are many things to write, not only to protest. And also you can make protest poetry against imperialism, capitalism, the bourgeoisie, military dictatorships in America and many other things. And also have a positive poem about the achievements of the revolution: the peasants receiving land, the literacy campaign, vaccinations, all those things are very poetic.

Alarcón: What about poetry critical of the Sandinista movement—is that possible now, positive criticism?

Cardenal: Well, we have poems against the revolution in the opposition paper, *La Prensa*. The government newspaper will not publish poems against the revolution. And *The New York Times* will not publish a communist poem, against capitalism. But in the opposition paper there is poetry against the revolution. We don't care about that.

Amirkhanian: What does the government do to assist artists?

Cardenal: We are promoting all the arts—poetry, painting, dance, crafts, folklore—through the Ministry of Culture. And they are promoted also with the union of writers and the theater artists union and the painters union and the musicians union.

Amirkhanian: Does the government give money to artists?

Cardenal: Not usually.

Amirkhanian: But they promote the arts.

Cardenal: Sometimes there is a very important writer that is in need and then there is a subvention from the government. A very important writer that is not able to make a living—maybe they have problems for instance, alcoholic or something like that, nobody will put them in a government position or in a diplomatic post or things like that—we want them to rehabilitate, just to write, so then they receive a subvention from the government.

Amirkhanian: Do artists have cultural exchanges with the Soviet Union?

Cardenal: Yes, not very much, but some Soviet writers have been there, and some of our writers have been in the Soviet Union. But also with many other countries—with East Germany and West Germany, and with Spain and France, with Mexico and Venezuela, Cuba, and with the United States also.

Kessler: How do you think North American poets can contribute to the struggle for peace in Central America?

Cardenal: The same as the churches in the United States, the trade unions, and university teachers and political organizations—I think the poets can also be important in our need of solidarity from the United States people.

Ferlinghetti: Most American poets are keeping silent. They can do the most for Nicaragua by speaking out, saying where they stand.

Cardenal: And by going to Nicaragua and seeing the good things about the revolution, and also the bad things, and telling here what they have seen.

1983

Passions of a Man:
Pasolini the Poet

Italian poet Pier Paolo Pasolini is best known in the United States as a filmmaker. Several years ago his scandalous *Saló: The 120 Days of Sodom*, an allegory of fascism adapted from a tale by the Marquis de Sade, aroused widespread outrage with the sickening violence of its subject matter. The film's notoriousness was typical of Pasolini's stormy romance (mostly in print) with the Italian public, but rarely had a respectable Yankee audience been confronted with the shocking honesty and self-revelation so disturbingly and perversely present in this movie.

Not long after *Saló* was made (in 1975), at the age of fifty-three, Pasolini was beaten to death by a young man under dubious and perhaps dirty circumstances. His infatuation with the beauty of boys and his history of erotic relations with them—as testified in his writings and suggested in many of his films (not always to artistic advantage, unless you're indiscriminately in love with young buns)—surrounded his death with rumors of obscene intentions for which the artist met a brutal end; in other words, he presumably made a pass at the wrong punk.

But at the time, Pasolini had been writing an incendiary

newspaper column in the *Corriere della Sera*, one of Italy's largest-circulation dailies, out of Milan. One hypothesis is that he may have been assassinated for the passion of his political diatribes rather than for his sexual persuasions. If his films and poems are any sign, his journalism must also have been fairly hair-raising. Pasolini surely had plenty of enemies; the brilliance and intensity of his mind and imagination were relentless.

My favorite film of his is *Pasolini's Decameron*, in which the director plays the part of the fourteenth-century painter Giotto who, in the course of creating a masterpiece mural, ransacks the local town and countryside for faces to place in his fresco. Each face naturally has a story behind it, which is where Boccaccio comes in with his *Decameron* to provide Pasolini with a literary classic he can use to his own purposes. *The Gospel According to Matthew* and the *Arabian Nights* were similarly reworked by Pasolini in the light of his own obsessions; in his version of Chaucer's *Canterbury Tales* the director plays the role of the poet, making a running joke of himself in the part.

In his *Decameron* Pasolini as the artist-possessed-by-art is so electrifying in the role of Giotto—a Giotto re-imagined by the actor and therefore all the more true-to-life by virtue of exaggeration—that the image of his face is unforgettable. As I recall, he scarcely says a word but his body's wiry springiness and the piercing look in his eye reflect a burning urgency of purpose—a purpose whose realization can come only through the *action* of art. His affectionately satirical treatment of human types in the *Decameron* is complemented by his comic portrait of himself as the driven maestro.

I'm thinking of Pasolini because a friend has sent me a copy of his *Poems*, published by Vintage in a bilingual paperback with superb translations by Norman MacAfee. This is the first major collection of Pasolini's poetry to appear in North America and it's a revelation. Author of more than forty books of poetry, fiction and cultural/social criticism, Pasolini is acknowledged in Europe as one of the century's leading writers. His literary works are late arriving on these shores partly no doubt due to the intricacy of his poetic technique and the difficulties it presents to any translator. But it wouldn't surprise me either if his Greco-romantic Marxism and the purple-to-red sexual/political edge of his sensibility also made him too hot for American publishers to handle. With this edition we're given less than a sixth of his output as a poet, but it's a beginning.

I hesitate to speak directly of the poems because any general observations that can be made don't come close to suggesting the power of Pasolini's voice. Part of this power derives from a paradoxical relation between the poet and his art: Pasolini, if we take his word for it, was tormented by the inherent limitation—a kind of cultural conservatism—implicit in any high literary tradition, of which he felt himself a perpetuator. He knew and revered the humanizing value of the great tradition while at the same time desiring the creative demolition of an otherwise dying culture.

Poetry, for Pasolini, had somehow to turn itself to "practical ends" in order to make a difference in a decadent and corrupt society. It had to become a living force or wither away among the rest of the artifacts with which the bourgeoisie fortifies its own vanity. The publication in national magazines of inflammatory poems like "The Italian Communist Party Speaks to the Young!!" (1968) made him a controversial figure in his country, but Pasolini was no simpleminded propagandist. The courage of his dialectical probe of reality is active in the very process of his writing so that within each poem there are consciousness-wrenching struggles going on between the contradictions in his own vision.

Resolving such contradictions through poetry is something any great poet might attempt, but Pasolini takes his art a step further by declaring its inadequacy to the task he sets it. If writing has no practical outcome, if it doesn't change the world, it is scarcely (yet none-the-less) worth doing. Pasolini's personal anguish and despair, the separateness he felt on account of his homosexuality and the tumultuousness of his genius, were equaled by a *religious* fervor for political transformation. His language, charged as it is with ancient and contemporary energies, faiths and doubts, embodies his inner battle so beautifully it assumes a certain tragic-heroic grace.

The wholly committed extremism, the "desperate vitality" of Pasolini's search for revolutionary expression is one measure of his integrity as an artist. The truthfulness and nakedness and pain throughout his poetry are moving because they're worked out in endlessly inventive progress toward an unattainable consummation: a sexual/social consummation which, if it ever could occur, would make the new society the greatest, most compassionate poem of all.

By throwing himself simultaneously into the epic drama of history, into the alley of lowlife adventure, into the mythology of the movies and the intellectual dignity of "the tradition," Pasolini may seem to have burnt himself out at a stake of his own making—but his poems endure and testify to his fire's continuing light.

1982

Theology for Atheists:
Yehuda Amichai's
Poetry of Paradox

Until his death last month in Jerusalem at the age of 76, Israeli poet Yehuda Amichai was a strong contender for the Nobel Prize in literature. His books translated into thirty-seven languages beyond the original Hebrew, Amichai has long been one of the planet's preeminent poets. The evidence in English is abundant, most notably up to now in two substantial volumes: *The Selected Poetry of Yehuda Amichai*, translated by Chana Bloch and Stephen Mitchell (Harper & Row, 1986; revised and expanded edition 1996, California), and *Yehuda Amichai: A Life of Poetry 1948–1994*, translated by Benjamin and Barbara Harshav (HarperCollins, 1994). As if that weren't enough, last spring we were given what the jacket flap touts as his magnum opus, a tightly integrated sequence of poems translated by Bloch and Chana Kronfeld, *Open Closed Open*.

Amichai is a connoisseur of the paradoxical. By turns, and often at the same time, erotic and metaphysical, devout and skeptical, earnest and ironic, grief-drenched and dryly witty, his poems investigate contemporary realities from a biblical perspective and rethink biblical stories from a contemporary angle. Jewish down to the bones, his humanity is broadly universal, obsessed as he is with time and death, war and peace, love and memory, joy and suffering. Zionist in his attachment to the rocks and sand of his homeland (Amichai emigrated to Palestine from Germany in 1936 at the age of twelve), still he is not a nationalist in the political sense of that word.

Rooted in the geography of the desert landscape, its physical details and sensations, its ancient and modern history, its cosmic mysteries, Amichai is also the most intimate of love poets, as passionately entangled with his woman as with his country. He finds in the lover's embrace both evidence of the divine and consolation for its absence. The human body—his own, his lover's—is a garden, a battlefield, a sanctuary, an oasis, a meeting place of the temporal and the eternal.

As a Jewish atheist Taoist existentialist, I am not favorably predisposed toward theological discourse. Religious orthodoxy of any kind, with its authoritarian overtones, tends to provoke my inner anarchist. But Amichai's poetry, religious as it undeniably is, cultivates such a shrewd irreverence and is so alive with insight, so earthy and individual, that it's irresistible even to a disbeliever. In a poem called "Gods Change, Prayers Are Here to Stay," he offers this lesson in comparative religion:

> The God of the Christians is a Jew, a bit of a whiner,
> and the God of the Muslims is an Arab Jew from the
>   desert, a bit hoarse.
> Only the God of the Jews isn't Jewish.
> The way Herod the Edomite was brought in to be king
>   of the Jews,
> so God was brought back from the infinite future,

> an abstract God: neither painting nor graven image nor
>   tree nor stone.

Is nothing sacred to this wise guy? Well, yes and no. Perhaps the poet's imagination is what it takes to revitalize exhausted dogma. A little further along in the same poem Amichai suggests this himself:

> We are all children of Abraham
> but also the grandchildren of Terah, Abraham's father.
> And maybe it's high time the grandchildren
> did unto the father as he did unto his
> when he shattered his idols and images, his religion,
>   his faith.
> That too would be the beginning of a new religion.

This sense of a faith at odds with itself, of a person wrestling with his own belief in search of spiritual truth, gives the religious dimension of Amichai's poetry far greater weight and resonance than more conventional affirmations of piety.

The political slant of these poems is even more elusive. Fraught with history, violence and the ongoing geopolitical (and theopolitical) arguments that have wracked his land since long before it was a Jewish state, they almost never address directly the "issues" we see debated in the newspapers. Unlike such leading Palestinian poets as Adonis and Mahmoud Darwish—who, exiled from their home and constantly trying to correct that loss, invoke a collective nostalgia, defiance and urgent thirst for justice—Amichai seems to see war and peace, terrorism and coexistence, even borders, as difficult realities endemic not only to the region but to the human condition. He reflects on his own combat experience, the fear and courage of soldiers, his son and daughter being drafted and disappearing on buses with their faces "in the corner of the window like a stamp on an envelope," and "the thud of the censor's seal like the hammerblow of fate," but the only explicit protest in his poetry—and even that is muted by a sigh of resignation—is not against the censor or any government or enemy, but against fate itself, or God, or whatever demonic force it is that causes humanity to lust for its own blood.

Like an archeologist, the poet excavates and sifts the sub-political evidence for clues to the deeper dynamics driving human conduct. "Jerusalem, Jerusalem, Why Jerusalem?" should be read by anyone seeking to understand why it's so vexing for any government—let alone two or three governments and as many religions—to resolve the question of who that city belongs to. "I always have to go in the opposite direction to whatever / is passing and past," he writes. "That's how I know I live in Jerusalem." Going "against the tide of pilgrims," swimming upstream against "the joy-parades," thriving on the principle of opposition, the poet is divided against his own people, who are in turn divided among, and sometimes within, themselves. How could he or anyone expect whole states to agree on anything?

As usual, it is the lovers who offer a glimpse of relief from such madness, albeit with their own brand of fanaticism:

> Two lovers talking to each other in Jerusalem
> with the excitement of tour guides, pointing,
> touching, explaining: These are my father's eyes
>   you see

in my face, these are the sleek thighs I inherited from a
     distant mother
in the Middle Ages, this is my voice which traveled
all the way here from three thousand years ago,
this is the color of my eyes, the mosaic of my spirit,
the archeological layers of my soul. We are holy places.

Is Amichai being allegorical? Could these lovers be Jew and
Arab? Are the bodies, animated by history and desire, mysti-
cally related to a body politic that might transcend hatred and
ideology, united by Eros—praise Allah, thank God, "amen and
may it come to pass"? Or is it only that he sees in sexual love a
kind of redemption, though not without its own struggles for
power and sovereignty?

The poignancy of our earthly sojourn, its ephemeral
sweetness, the pregnancy of the smallest human gestures, the
haunted beauty and richness of the most mundane things and
events—none of this is lost on the poet. He dares to tackle cosmic themes in domestic terms, as in "Houses (Plural); Love
(Singular)":

We lived in many houses and left remnants of
     memory
in every one of them: a newspaper, a book face-
     down, a crumpled map
of some faraway land, a forgotten toothbrush
     standing sentinel in a cup—
that too is a memorial candle, an eternal light.

If even a toothbrush, in Amichai's universe, can be a sacred object, how much more sacred then must be the hand that holds the toothbrush, and the lovers' hands caressing one another, and the disembodied memories themselves and the minds remembering. With Amichai, ripples of implication set out from the simplest phrases and spread indefinitely.

His lines are almost prosaic in their conversational quality, and yet they are subtly rhythmic, lyric, layered with associations. I don't read Hebrew, but in these English versions by Bloch and Kronfeld I feel I am getting the mood, the tone, the pace, the punning wit, the linguistic mischievousness of the original, or as close an approximation as one could hope for. They catch, in colloquial English, the contradictory currents and emotional riptides under the calm surface of Amichai's measured voice.

"Real meaning, for Amichai," Bloch and Kronfeld wrote recently in *The American Poetry Review*, "resides not in language...but in the 'soul-stutterings' of human emotion." It must be that subterranean stutter that paradoxically informs these expert translators' eloquence in representing not just the words but the spirit of this extraordinary poet.

2000

Guy Davenport's
Greek Revival

Without the benefit of a classical education and lacking the intellectual discipline of a true Rexrothian autodidact, my knowledge of the great Greek poets is limited to the excellence of a few key modern translations: Richmond Lattimore's thunderous *Iliad* with its clattering consonants; the lofty melodious narrative sinews of Robert Fitzgerald's *Odyssey*; Mary Barnard's lucid musical reconstructions of Sappho; Dudley Fitts's hip and witty 1938 versions of the Greek Anthology poems (issued in paperback by New Directions in 1956, long out of print)—all ancient and up-to-date at the same time, proving again Pound's famous dictum that all ages are contemporaneous. Now New Directions has added another title to this short list of classics: *7 Greeks*, Guy Davenport's compilation of all the available fragments of seventh- to third-century-BC poets and thinkers Archilochos, Sappho, Alkman, Anakreon, Herakleitos, Diogenes and Herondas. The book is a treasure, a marvelously mixed assortment ranging from the passionately lyrical to the coolly satirical, all rendered with the precise grace of Davenport's interpretive touch.

What has always moved me most about the old Greeks, so evident in Fitts's renditions and here again in Davenport's, is their naked immediacy of expression—emotional honesty without sentimentality—the instinct to cut through everything right to the heart of meaning. In philosophers Herakleitos and Diogenes this economy derives from a concentration on essentials. Even though both are pre- or anti-Platonic, they're pursuing a pure truth, a sense of absolutes arrived at by observation and intuition rather than elaborate rhetorical logic. Herakleitos resembles no one so much as Lao Tzu; the Greek's portable aphorisms are a natural (and near-contemporary) companion volume to the Chinese sage's *Tao Te Ching*. Diogenes is more social critic than metaphysician, yet his scathing observations on his immediate milieu apply equally to our time and place as to his. Poets Sappho and Anakreon confront directly the agonies of desire and mortality with an urgency, however artfully wrought, that trumps esthetics. Archilochos, both singer and soldier, combines the passion of Sappho with the jaded worldliness of Diogenes—a powerful combination. "I yearn," writes Sappho, "And I hunt." The art of these verbal hunters is as necessary as the paintings in the Altamira caves; it serves the purpose of spiritual nutrition: the maker's survival depends on it.

In addition to their urgent necessity, another reason for the tightness of these texts undoubtedly has to do with the fact that in many cases fragments are all we have. Yet a single surviving line from one of Sappho's pieces—"Asleep against the breasts of a friend." "You make me hot." "More valuable than gold."— resonates endlessly in the surrounding silence. Lamentable as it may be to have lost the wholeness of so many splendid poems, the existing fragments have proved a trove for investigative translators. Davenport's versions are masterly: elegantly spare, evocative, musical, speakable. Sometimes he provides alternate readings to demonstrate the *approximate* nature of translation, showing how very different strategies can comparably render original meanings. And many of the pieces, in their epigrammatic brevity, pierce the reader's awareness with painful one-liner wit, as in this fragment of Archilochos:

> It's not your enemies
> But your friends
> You've got to watch.

Ironically, the one overtly comic writer presented in *7 Greeks*, Herondas, whose satiric mimes the translator sees as related to the monologues of Lily Tomlin—"farces deliciously rendered by a master impersonator of types"—strikes me as the least funny, most dated, most easily forgotten section of the book. Perhaps it is the performance-oriented, stagey quality of the skits that makes them seem so out of place among the deeper thinkers and singers, but it may be also that the savage mockery of Archilochos and Diogenes simply makes the more superficial satire look frivolous. As Nietzsche, a scholar and admirer of the early Greeks, was later to prove, a great philosopher is likely to be much funnier than a good comedian. Herondas may have been the Lenny Bruce of his time, but in this collection, alongside the other, more soulful musings, his jokes fall flat even as they give the translator a chance to demonstrate another side of his stylistic virtuosity.

Similarly Davenport's four different versions of Alkman's "Hymn to Artemis of the Strict Observance"—a tour de force of the translator's art in its multiple readings of an incomplete text, ranging from the more or less literal to the totally speculative—may be of interest to the scholar of Greek verse but feel to me less deeply moving than most of the rest of the book. This may be just my personal preference for the lyric or aphoristic mode over the more ritualized formality of Alkman's hymn "For a Chorus of Spartan Girls Dressed as Doves to Sing at Dawn on the Feast of the Plow," but the highly stylized voice of the poet here feels to me quaintly antiquated rather than emotionally compelling.

But five out of seven isn't a bad average. While I'm less engaged by Alkman and Herondas, the others, each in a distinctive way, unfold their pleasures and powers over and over. Best known to our time, and most translated, is the sublime Sappho, one of whose fragments, rendered here twice by Davenport, could serve as a self-portrait:

> There are none like her,
> And none will ever see the light of the sun,
> None hereafter will have that mastery.

Or, alternately:

> I cannot believe there is any girl
> Under the sun, or shall be to come,
> With an intelligence like hers.

For those who object to sexual objectification, Sappho may present problems. Her lust could hardly be more explicit and, in the political context of our own contemporary sex wars, could probably be seen by the gender police as a violation of the individuality of the (mostly) girls for whose bodies she hungers.

Yet we have here also the idealization, far more ethereal than pornographic, of physical beauty at its most alluring:

> I put here, my lazy girl, this soft cushion,
> And if, with your blouse off, in your soft arms.

Or again:

> And your boy's beauty,
> What else is so trim, so lithe,
> Impetuous follower?
> Straight slender trees
> Have that balance.

Sappho's fixation on physical grace has a moral dimension equally profound:

> Beauty is for the eyes and fades in a while,
> But goodness is a beauty that lasts forever.

In these "complete" fragments we find the synthesis that moves the poet to song. A beautiful body may be exciting, but a beautiful body combined with a beautiful mind is more thrilling still, and in turn the source of the greatest grief:

> Eros weaver of myths,
> Eros sweet and bitter,
> Eros bringer of pain.

What poet hasn't attempted these themes? Song, the lyric impulse, springs from desire. In all the years since Sappho it's hard to name a singer more finely tuned to the eye's delight, the heart's longing, the sharp intelligence of the senses. Davenport's freshly wrought versions, while not surpassing Barnard's in sparkling clarity, give us access to the original from yet another angle, proving that even the simplest lines, if deep enough in their art, are inexhaustible.

Closest of these to Sappho in emotional nakedness is Anakreon. As Sappho is drawn to the loveliness of girls, Anakreon idealizes and desires boys, but to read either as merely "homoerotic" is to reduce their universality. Consider this self-contained couplet:

> I love it when we play together.
> You do it with such grace and verve.

Maybe this is sexual—homo or hetero—maybe not, but whatever its "orientation" may be, there's no escaping its sexiness. Or for blueslike poignancy:

> Lovely, too lovely,
> And too many love you.

Davenport's light touch allows the natural weight of such utterances to resound with all its heartbreaking implications. Yet Anakreon is not all sweetness and love; he has an edge—

> Silence, O God,
> Those who speak
> Such awful Greek.

—and an ironic consciousness of his own erotic vulnerability:

> I am perhaps in love

Again, perhaps not,
And crazy to boot.
No, not crazy.

The playful earnestness, or earnest playfulness, of such reflections adds to their gravity even as it lightens their underlying anguish.

Archilochos takes both anguish and irony to extremes. A professional soldier tempered by the ferocities of the battlefield, his poems have both a steely hardness and—just when you thought he was a tough guy—moments of the tenderest sensitivity. At one end of the spectrum he declares with a mixture of bitterness and disgust:

Like Odysseus under the ram
You have clung under your lovers
And under your love of lust,
Seeing nothing else for this mist,
Dark of heart, dark of mind.

Or in a similar vein:

His attachment to the despicable
Is so affectionate and stubborn,
Argument can't reach him.

But then again:

How many times,
How many times,
On the gray sea,
The sea combed

By the wind
Like a wilderness
Of woman's hair,
Have we longed,
Lost in nostalgia,
For the sweetness
Of homecoming.

Or more simply and touchingly still:

And the heart
Is pleased
By one thing
After another.

Again these are entire poems, or fragments, whose concise wholeness stands alone eloquently with no need for exegesis; they mean exactly what they say. The translator's work feels both spontaneous and polished, a transparent window into the original.

If Archilochos comes across as a tough guy with a sometimes tender heart, Diogenes the cosmopolitan misanthrope admits to no such qualifications. A homeless vagabond who prefers the company of dogs to that of men, he is the original Cynic whose cutting wit and lack of illusions enable him not only to see through every kind of social hypocrisy but to say what he knows without concern for the consequences. "Of what use is a philosopher," he asks, "who doesn't hurt anybody's feelings?" Diogenes was a slave and what we would call a street person, but the furthest thing from any kind of victim. He describes himself as "an exiled beggar dressed in rags:

wise, independent, and content." He has freed himself from the miseries of desire by means of philosophy, which "can turn a young man from the love of a beautiful body to the love of a beautiful mind." He understands the wealth of poverty: "To own nothing is the beginning of happiness." And he knows the value of education: "There is no stick hard enough to drive me away from a man from whom I can learn something." There are one hundred twenty-four such zingers in Davenport's gathering, and at least half of them are the kind of gems that are not just easy to memorize but can also serve as guides to conduct, understanding, consolation. Wisdom cannot be had from another's words, one must gain it through lived experience; but the words of a seasoned thinker like Diogenes can confirm—or challenge—one's own emerging or assumed sense of what matters and what doesn't. "The greatest beauty of human kind is frankness," he declares. Discomfiting as some of them may be, his timeless maxims offer shelter from our current hurricanes of dubious information.

Herakleitos offers a more metaphysical yet equally illuminating wisdom. If the perspective of Diogenes is earthy, that of Herakleitos is cosmic. Echoes of his cosmology can be heard in Ecclesiastes ("All things come in seasons."), in Taoist and Zen teachings ("Joints are and are not parts of the body."), in Blake's Proverbs of Hell ("The beautifullest harmonies come from opposition."), in William Carlos Williams ("Men who wish to know about the world must learn about it in its particular details."); Hopkins, one of the greatest Catholic poets, openly subscribes to the pagan concept of nature's "Heraclitean Fire"; in the opening paragraph of *The Adventures of Augie March* Saul Bellow invokes the Heraclitean notion that character is fate; Elias Canetti in his notebooks refers to Herakleitos as one of his model philosophers; W. S. Merwin uses Herakleitos's parable of Homer and children catching lice as the epigraph for one of his best books. The list could go on. The man was attuned to universal truths. And yet for all their metaphysical currency, his epigrams can also, like those of Diogenes, cut through contemporary social questions as if written in response to the latest newscast: "Bigotry is the disease of the religious." Or: "Justice stalks the liar and the false witness." Again, of one hundred twenty-four self-explanatory sayings (some given two or three ways), at least half are the kind of touchstone teachings anyone half-awake will want to return to again and again, if only to be reminded: "One ought not to talk or act as if he were asleep."

In the miasma of current publishing, swamped as we are with more new books than we can possibly stay aware of much less read, 7 *Greeks* is a gift, one of those rare volumes that has a certain vital inevitability laced through its pages. Whether one reads it for insight into the culture of "the oldest dead white European males" (in Bernard Knox's good-natured phrase), for the esthetic pleasure of its poetry, for instruction in how to live, for creative inspiration, or for solace—these people suffered the same or worse than you and turned it to deathless art—the book is a reservoir of wonder and strength. Only through a translator of Davenport's instincts, learning, genius, care and skill would we have these works in such accessible, finely wrought, up-to-the-minute form. And for his efforts he deserves our gratitude.

1996

Czeslaw Milosz,
1911–2004

Czeslaw Milosz, Polish poet, 1980 Nobel Laureate and long-time professor at UC Berkeley, died at his home in Krakow this past August. He was ninety-three, had lived through three world wars (counting the Cold War), had chosen exile over the intellectual compromises required by communism, found himself for some thirty years improbably stranded in the strange paradise of California, and returned to die in his native land and language. In addition to his prolific contributions as a novelist, essayist, editor, critic and translator, Milosz was without doubt one of the greatest poets of the twentieth century.

Like many mid-century East Europeans caught between the contending forces of Nazism and Stalinism—and their respective armies—Milosz had no illusions about the latent darkness in human character. His poetry, tinged with a sober historical pessimism, nevertheless affirms the sweetness of experience in the wonders of love, sex, all the senses, the specific and multiple astonishments of being alive on earth. The cruelty and stupidity and cowardice and corruption he witnessed as his country was overrun and occupied by one totalitarian utopia and then another infused his writings with a grave authority and a darkly ironic and tragic sense of the human predicament. As a witness to historic atrocities and displacements, he never let himself off the hook by claiming innocence, but rather acknowledged his complicity, by virtue of his very existence, in the mess man has made of things.

At his readings in California, a couple of which I attended, Milosz seemed weary and deeply skeptical as to whether these childlike Americans in their relative innocence could possibly understand what he was talking about. But the poems, never easy or simpleminded, consistently struck me with their beauty and profundity—passionately intelligent investigations into what it means to live in this world. He was the opposite of a crowd pleaser: With terrible honesty and devastating insight he forced us to face the most disturbing truths while somehow transforming that confrontation into a celebration of integrity and endurance.

Milosz was a strikingly handsome man, even well into his seventies. With his flying eyebrows, erect bearing, well-tailored suits and richly accented English, he cut an imposing figure—an Old World gentleman, tough-minded but never jaded, who knew what he had to do and did it with extraordinary commitment. His work in the largest sense was to carry forward the great European literary tradition into the most atrocious of centuries and renew it using the very horrors of the era as an invigorating ingredient of his vision, converting what could have been an occasion for nihilism into a source of liberating insight.

His publications in English run to more than two dozen volumes of verse, prose, translations and anthologies. In whatever form he employed the writing was lucid, challenging, confident, touched with both lyrical and intellectual grace. Wherever you open any one of his books you find an exacting mind that invites you to rise to its level and engage a glimmer of its brilliance. The great gift of Milosz's work outlives the man, whose many years and written record trace a life of tremendous energy, courage and difficult wisdom.

2004

Back Home

What Does It Take
to Translate Poetry?

"In theory, only poets should translate poetry; in reality, poets are seldom good translators." So writes Octavio Paz in his essay "Translation: Literature and Literality." The master goes on to explain: "They are not [good translators] because they almost always use the foreign poem as a point of departure for writing their own poem."

This ranks, along with Robert Frost's much-quoted witticism that what gets lost in translation of a poem is the poetry, as one of the great red herrings—and most abused anecdotes—of translation folklore. Paz himself, in the same paragraph, hedges his bets by declaring with equal authority: "The good translator of poetry is a translator who is, in addition, a poet—like Arthur Waley; or a poet who is, in addition, a good translator—like Nerval when he translated *Faust Part I*."

So which is it? Do poets make the best translators or not? As anyone with any sense can tell, it depends on the poet. Paz and Frost are setting up straw men and mowing them down with the force of their own rhetoric. For Paz, the typical poet is an egomaniac unable to put himself at the service of anyone else's poem; for Frost, the translator is a feckless scribe who may understand the language but lacks the skill and grace to turn a poem into a poem.

Both these stereotypes, while true up to a point, are equally irrelevant to the practicing translator. As countless masterpieces of translation testify, the poet need not be in it only to advance his own agenda, and the translator need not be a tin-eared imitator hopelessly inferior to the original artist. Paz deepens his discussion by explaining the dialectical opposition he finds between the ways in which poets and translators work: "When writing, the poet doesn't know how his poem will turn out; when translating, the translator knows his poem should reproduce the poem before his eyes." Thus, he concludes, "translation is a parallel operation, though in reverse, to poetic creation."

So: Must a translator of poetry be a poet? This sounds to me like a trick question, or maybe a Zen koan—akin to: Must a ballerina be a dancer? Must a pianist be a musician? Must an actor be a performer? Or perhaps most trickily, Must a bear shit in the woods?

Well, some bears shit in the zoo. Polar bears presumably shit in the snow of the tundra. But where else except in the woods do most bears shit? Surely the same logic applies to the vast majority of ballet dancers, pianists and actors. Who else is qualified to execute the demanding moves of those rigorous disciplines? So there must be something more to this question about translators and poets. Some subtext only an exegete might unlock. But what?

Translation is a kind of exegesis. In order for a translator to open a poem into a new language, he or she must understand the meaning of the text. An astute scholar or critic with sufficient knowledge of the original language may well be able to tease out the meanings of even the most obscure, ambiguous, esoteric or irrational poem. He (I use the masculine pronoun for convenience) may well be able to paraphrase the poem and to expound on its themes, its structure, its technique, its style, even its vision; he may even be able to transcribe accurately the words of the poem such that its meanings will be somewhat discernible.

But a poem, more than almost any other kind of text, means exactly what it says and what can't be said in any other way, even as its language may shimmer with multiplicity. To bring the poem alive in another language means, yes, to lose the original poetry; but it can also mean to regain new qualities implicit in the original, resulting in an analogous experience for the reader. To make the new poem live on the page and make its sounds move musically in the air with something resembling its original spirit requires a very particular combination of skills; and those skills, and the sensibility to deploy them with the necessary nuance, belong primarily to a class of writers commonly known as poets.

Literary translation is writing. Translators at the top level of the art are specialists equipped with the tools and training to execute their task, and the most fundamental discipline they must master is that of writing. In the case of poetry translators, it goes without saying—but it needs to be said anyway—that the poet's tools and the knowledge of how to use them are indispensable.

Even a non-poet, when he's translating, is necessarily a poet. When he's laying those lines of ink down on the page, his dictionaries open on the desk, his full attention brought to bear on the text—its blatant significations and its mysteries—with any luck or grace he may feel possessed by the poem's author, may feel as if he is channeling the voice in the poem and so, in this moment of re-composition or re-creation, in the zone or flow of inspired translation, even in the analytical rigor of a more rational procedure, this writer who may seldom if ever compose original verse of his own is, by virtue of what he's doing now, a poet.

But like the musician who in the flow of performance may feel possessed or directed by the pre-existing composition, the series of notes laid down by the composer, or the actor completely absorbed in a written character, the poetry translator needs not only the sensibility but the technique and imagination to bring the work to fruition. Technique because, as should be obvious, the laws of prosody inevitably come into play in the re-composing of a poem—all the subtleties of sound and rhythm, measure and rhyme (in the largest sense of pattern and correspondence, not just the mechanical sound that lands at the end of a line like the bell on the carriage return of a manual typewriter)—and only a poet practiced in the intricacies of the art can reliably make a translation in anything resembling its original music.

Technique and imagination. Understanding the language of the original is helpful and often important, though not necessarily essential; there are numerous examples of poets who collaborate with linguists and scholars of idioms they don't know, or assemble from earlier versions, or versions in other languages, what might be called synthetic interpretations. Yet there are countless bilingual or multilingual individuals, even highly sensitive and literate ones, people exceedingly capable of understanding what they read in another language, who couldn't translate a poem to save their lives. And why is this? Well, for one thing, they don't "speak Poetry." And I would add, with all respect, they are not practiced in the poet's art, which entails, among other receptive and active traits, the art of listening.

A poet must be attuned to the sounds of lines taking form in the mind, and in finding the precise words and phrases to trace the faintest hint of a thought or feeling through its linguistic texture into a shape on the page and a sound in the air that somehow approaches the elusive music implied as the words emerge from their pre-conscious source. The poet learns this ineffable skill of careful listening not in a workshop or through instruction but by reading as deeply as possible as much great poetry as possible and appropriating, by keen attention and imitation, the habits of hearing patterns of sound and rhymes and ideas and images, the particular rhythms and thoughts-in-progress that somehow, inexplicably, amount to poetry.

This is not a field for the faint of heart, though anyone is free to try their hand and can learn a lot from the process. Many poets have used translation as a way to increase and extend the scope of their own poetic potential. And certainly there are examples of nonpoet translators who, through patient practice over years, develop the sensibility and skills to create very fine versions of the poets they translate—this elite group would include the likes of Clare Cavanaugh, Robert Fagles, John Felstiner, Alexis Levitin and Eliot Weinberger, among others. But these are exceptions. The vast majority of successful translators—and by successful I don't mean in terms of fame but rather full realization in English of what they translate—are poets on their own time. Not necessarily well-known or "successful" poets in the conventional sense, but writers whose lives have been lived in the service of poetry. Many of the best translators have been less than major poets, poets whose original writings may be scarcely known beyond a small circle of readers (I think of Arthur Waley, Robert Fitzgerald, Mary Barnard, William Arrowsmith, David Ferry, Guy Davenport, Willis Barnstone, Alastair Reid, Chana Bloch and Roger Greenwald, to name a few), but poets nonetheless.

And then there are the poets known for their own original writings—poets like Ezra Pound and Kenneth Rexroth, W. S. Merwin and Robert Bly, Anne Carson and Clayton Eshleman— who have also made important contributions as translators. In the case of some, most notably Pound and Bly, the force of their own poetic personality or voice may overwhelm that of whatever poet they happen to be translating and, as Paz observed, the original poet becomes subsumed in the poet/translator's style. But the greatest translators subscribe to Keats's notion of the poet as "the most unpoetical thing in existence," as having no identity of his own, the better to adapt to the voice of whatever happens to be using him as a medium.

Merwin, for example, surely one of the master poets of our time, and one of the most ubiquitously published and garlanded with prizes, whose personal signature in his original writing is utterly distinctive, also has the uncanny ability as a translator to vanish within or behind the voice of whoever he happens to be translating. Perhaps his Buddhist practice has something to do with the egolessness of his nonpersona, his invisibility, as a translator, but he was a first-rate translator before he was a Buddhist, and I think this is a function of his mastery of prosody (which in turn may be largely due to his early and extensive training in translation).

Jack Hirschman, another prolific poet/translator, who works with astonishing speed and versatility from at least a half-dozen languages, because of the velocity and spontaneity of his practice can often be found to have made mistakes in his haste. But the poems consistently sound like poems in vital American English, and thanks to Hirschman's poetic genius the flavor if not the letter of the original is brought across for the listener or reader to experience.

Which brings us to the question of accuracy—of what it is, exactly, and how important to the larger issue of fidelity. Gregory Rabassa, arguably the greatest translator of Latin American fiction (yet not a fiction writer himself), has spoken of the critic he calls Professor Horrendo. Professor Horrendo, a scholar of languages, like many academics is fixated on correctness, and in the case of translation, being correct means being accurate. But what is accuracy? Is it getting right the dictionary definition of every word in the original? Every specific image? Must it serve as a functional paraphrase of the poem's themes or ideas? Or is it something less measurable, something no dictionary, no scholar, no computer can define? (We've only begun to see the comic results of Google's Universal Library, where in some techno-utopian future, at the click of a button, works of literature will be instantly translated into any language desired.)

One thing I believe a poet is more likely to understand than other translators, human or robotic, is that in translation "accuracy" is really the least of one's problems. Fidelity is a far more important matter, and it is a matter of mood and tone and nuance, of atmosphere and rhythm and timing, of melody and feeling and all the elusive, ineffable elements that separate a work of art from one of craft or mechanics. When you look across the page from a great translation at the original and compare the literal meaning of the words with what the translator has written, your response is less likely to be "Wow, that's really accurate!" than "Wow, how did he ever think to come up with that?"

The difference between these two types of translation is imagination. The one of whom you ask how he came up with that is the one who has mobilized his imagination, not just his knowledge of languages but his gift for finding analogies, to re-create the poem in an English that approximates the feeling, the sense, the meaning—beyond the correctly conveyed words—of the original. Imagination is the poet's realm, and it is through imagination (or faithful re-imagination) that the greatest translations are created.

The art of translation, like the art of poetry, is open to anyone. No formal permit or license is required. You just, as Frank O'Hara put it, go on your nerve. In time, with practice, patience and perseverance, one may develop the moves, the intuition, the ear, the stylistic versatility and virtuosity, the range, the technique, the confidence, the humility, the daring, the presumption, the gifted accomplishment of skilled translation. It's possible, I suppose, to do this by reading and translating fulltime and without ever publishing a line of original poetry. But in my experience the motivation to write and the motive to translate are intertwined, if not one and the same: the desire to bring something true and beautiful and unique and revelatory into the world. The practice of one is inextricably bound up with the other, and one feeds the other and enhances it in what Paz calls "a continual and mutual fertilization."

Must a translator of poetry be a poet? Maybe not. But if not, he has to be able to do a very persuasive impersonation of one.

2007

Forgery & Possession:
The Poet as Translator

"Some people think that translating poetry must be difficult,"
W. S. Merwin remarked to a meeting of the American Literary
Translators Association in the early 1980s in New Orleans.
"But we know that's not true. It's impossible." Only a virtuoso
poet/translator of Merwin's accomplishment would have the
authority and the humility to acknowledge such a bedrock
artistic truth while proceeding in his work, time after time, to
disprove it. And this paradox is at the heart of any translator's
practice. For to bring a poem from one idiom (one culture,
one individual vision) into another is literally to write a new
poem. That's why no two translations of the same poem are
ever exactly alike.

A number of skills and concepts must be mobilized in this
impossible but necessary enterprise. Being bilingual helps, of
course, but is in itself far from sufficient. Familiarity with the
culture and history of the original is also vitally useful. And a
certain amount of scholarship regarding biographical context,
linguistic and literary allusions, and the whole historic ambi-
ence surrounding the text is helpful and important, up to a

point. Still, I would argue that the skills of a poet are most instrumental in enabling a poem to be moved successfully from one language to another, new one—such skills and gifts as technical control, a live imagination, a musical ear, negative capability (Keats's poetic principle of being able to "live in uncertainty" and to speak from the point of view of other identities than one's own), courage, humility, a kind of presumptuousness, a keen intelligence, an aptitude for unlikely associations, emotional sensitivity, linguistic instinct, and an actor's empathy and powers of impersonation.

When I first started translating, as a young poet in the late 1960s and early 1970s, it was as much an exercise in reading as in writing. Most existing translations that I could find, at the time, of such Spanish-language poets as Machado, García Lorca, Alberti and Neruda seemed somehow slightly off—not necessarily "inaccurate" but out of tune—and I wanted to hear for myself how some of those poems would sound in my own American English, in the hope that that would help me understand them. Academic scholars may scoff, but translation of a foreign text into one's own idiom is about the deepest reading one can do: in the process of physically absorbing and transforming the original into the new language you may gain a far more profound understanding than that afforded by the most rigorous critical analysis. By the time you finish translating a poem you know it as if you had written it yourself—and in a very real sense, you have. (Not that the poet always knows best what he or she has put into a poem, but that's a subject for another discussion.)

I soon discovered, in the course of translating many Neruda poems, and then the more difficult texts of Vicente Aleixandre, that translation was also a tremendously helpful workshop in practical prosody: I had to learn to mimic the verbal moves of these masters, and in so doing was extending the range of my own linguistic and poetic skills. Imitating the long lines of Aleixandre's poems in order to render them faithfully in a roughly analogous English was as exacting, in its technical demands, as my teenage efforts at mastering the sonnet. By placing myself at the service of the maestro I was at the same time developing habits that would be of use in my original writing.

As, over the years, translation has become a more and more integral part of my writing life, I've found—especially in those periods when I haven't had much to say in my own poetry—that translating others not only keeps my technical licks in tune but also enables me to write on themes and inhabit sensibilities to which I might not otherwise have access. And so the more "selfless" or "impersonal" act of translating ends up enriching the more intimate effort to speak in a distinctively personal voice. The dialectic is vital to both sides of the exchange, and at best it benefits the work of poet and translator alike.

Here's where the question of influence inevitably arises. When you immerse yourself in the work of another poet—even as a reader, but especially as a translator charged with assuming the other poet's persona—how much of that poet's voice and vision end up infecting your own? And conversely, how does your personal style and linguistic signature color what you do with those of another poet? While ideally a translator's style should be transparent, letting the original shine through undistorted, every poet who translates does, to one degree or another, make the original over in his or her own image. When the affinity between both poets is a natural fit, this switch of identities may be just what the poem calls for. At other times the change can be disastrous. There are countless examples of poet/translators whose own personalities interpose themselves between the original poet and the reader in such a way that the original is more obscured than illuminated. This kind of translator-to-poet "influence" is less than edifying.

The other side of the question is even trickier. I think the younger we are as writers the more easily we are influenced by what we read (and translate) and therefore the poets whose work we engage in our formative years undoubtedly affect our own. There is a danger, I think, in devoting oneself exclusively to the translation of a single poet before one has established an independent style. But in my experience translating has been much the same as reading, in terms of influence: those writers whose work has most moved me, the ones I've spent the most time with, the ones I've engaged at the deepest levels of my being, are the ones whose influence I hope I've absorbed—not in the sense of stylistic imitation but more in a way of apprehending the world, in ways of seeing and listening and turning those perceptions into my own music. Most of all, the examples of so many distinctive individual voices saying things in their poems in precisely their own ways have given me courage to trust my deepest instincts to let my voice be heard and felt from a faithful, intimate place, regardless of how that may be received by others.

Of course there's something to be said for imitation, too. Like those painters I've seen in European museums meticulously copying the works of masters, mimicking great poems—either by translating them or interpretively writing "after" them—can be a functional step on the road to finding one's own style. Once one has mastered a broad enough range of poetic techniques, one ought to be equipped to do practically anything the muses demand. Translation itself is at best a kind of forgery, where the untrained eye or ear can't distinguish between the copy and what it's modeled on. The most deceptively effective translations are those that sound so true and right that they give the illusion, like all great poems, of arising from silence through necessity into inevitability.

While some important poets have also been major translators—Merwin, Pound and Rexroth, for example—there are many poets of lesser accomplishment in their own right whose translations are exemplary, even classic: Arthur Waley's Chinese, William Arrowsmith's Pavese, Robert Fitzgerald's Homer, Mary Barnard's Sappho, David Ferry's Horace and Alastair Reid's Borges, among numerous others. This suggests that for some of us, even if we're not destined for immortality, the translation of greater writers than ourselves can be a way to realize our own potential. The act of translating can evoke in us creative powers we might not otherwise know we had. We can make a contribution to literature while enlarging our own artistic accomplishment.

But as a poet/translator colleague of mine observed, one ironic aspect of this opportunity to make a self-transcending contribution is that in putting our skills at the service of these larger literary figures, our own independent achievement may be overshadowed. Known primarily as the translator of some eminent foreign poet, an American writer, especially in the current publishing climate, may find his or her original work ignored, or at least diminished in comparison. This speaks to the matter of one's so-called career, a subject that everyone who writes thinks about but which is considered unseemly to discuss in public. I've never personally felt that conflict of interest my colleague spoke of; I don't see how whatever I've done as a translator, especially if it's any good, could hurt my reputation as a poet. If anything, the visibility one can attain as a successful translator tends, I think, to increase one's credibility as a writer, even if that doesn't translate into book sales or critical acclaim. People respect others who do things well, and to achieve a certain level of artistry as a translator (though that may mean making yourself invisible in the work) can only enhance one's profile as a poet. Your poems finally live or die on their own.

More inspiring to me than the career question is the concept of an international fellowship of poets, who extend the reach of each other's writings by constantly turning them into new languages, finding new readers, reviving the value of the solitary labor that sooner or later may reach kindred souls on some other side of the world. Poetry and translation in this respect can feel like an evangelical enterprise whose mission may not exactly be one of espousing any particular orthodoxy or saving souls but of amazing people or setting off little verbal explosions in their consciousness, enriching life all around through the much-underestimated power of the word. Doing translation can make one feel like a very urbane guerrilla, undermining, transcending and generally subverting conventional apprehensions of reality.

Who hasn't felt, when reading Sappho or Tu Fu or Rilke or Milosz or Borges in translation, an unsettling sensation of having to rethink everything, question your assumptions, pay more attention to what's in front of you. As a translator you are given the privilege of being an instrument for this sort of revelation. Just writing the new words of the other poem in English is vigorous conditioning for whatever may follow on your own time. What you learn in the process sooner or later shows up, in one form or another, in anything else you do, on or off paper. Writing one's own poems, after all, is an act of translation, taking unspoken dictation from some other mysterious source and setting it down in language sufficient to what it feels like it means.

So translation benefits the translator—except perhaps where time is concerned. Jobs and family demands aside, some writers thrive on many simultaneous projects, moving from one to another the way a percussionist dances among his various drums and chimes and rattles and mallets and cymbals and brushes in the course of some extended performance, each sound contributing its timing or counterpoint or harmony to the others. But there are also those who zero in on a single work with intense focus until it's finished. For people who find time to be finite, the question of how to divide it among one's various loves and obligations can mean that part of one's passion must be sacrificed. With certain prolific exceptions, there's only so much a person can do in a day. Even so, in my experience the more I'm doing in one area the more I seem to be inspired in the others, as if writing and translating, poetry and prose, essays and editing weren't mutually exclusive or even separate but mutually reinforcing and all part of the same creative continuum.

As we discover different voices in ourselves by way of poets in other languages, we contain more multitudes from which to draw the inspiration and vision that make the work worthwhile. Translation can be a way of finding voices for our own inarticulate obsessions. We are plunged into mysteries we may not have known were haunting us. As in writing our own poems, we are forced to confront aspects of ourselves we may not have wanted to acknowledge. Translation, both doing it and reading its results, keeps pushing back the boundaries, moving our expedition farther across the frontier, deeper into the interior.

I would imagine that translators who don't write poems themselves also feel this exploratory sensation when bringing the foreign poet's lines into their own idiom. Although they may not think of themselves as poets, during the time they're translating poems I don't see how they can escape being poets: The successful translator of poetry, however modestly he or she proceeds with that humble task, by some strange alchemy becomes a poet in the process. They are possessed by the other poet, channeling that voice, which originates somewhere far beyond the page where the words are printed. This sense of possession, which biographers sometimes speak of, is one of the more spooky and exciting aspects of the translator's task; we have to remain open to being taken over by forces we don't understand. I'm sure this happens even to translators who wouldn't presume to call themselves poets; if not, they may be in the wrong line of work.

A poet of my acquaintance, tormented by the compulsion to transcribe the voices in his head, used to speak of poetry as a disease. After more than thirty years of living with this disorder I would amend his diagnosis to say that it's also a treatment, if not a cure, whose healing powers science has yet to explain. If translation is a medium of transmission—the way songs played over the radio are sometimes said to be "infectious"—those of us who engage in such high-risk behavior are assuming a grave and heady responsibility. Poetry is contagious, and the translator's job is to catch it and spread it around.

2000

Poetry & Radio:
A Sound Conspiracy

Once the artist was surrounded by a conspiracy of silence.
The modern artist is surrounded by a conspiracy of noise.

JEAN COCTEAU

In Jean Cocteau's film *Orpheus* (1950) the poet/protagonist receives his "inspiration" from a radio in the dashboard of his car. One of the most versatile and prolific artists of the twentieth century, Cocteau consistently proclaimed the strange otherness of imagination, the intimate yet alien nature of the creative force. The poet is given the language of his art from "the other world" and is responsible for bringing it across faithfully into this one. Most people do not normally hear this language and it's the poet's job to intermediate. The other voice is the source; the poet creates nothing.

American poet Jack Spicer took Cocteau's image further and proposed the concept of the poet *as* radio, receiving signals from elsewhere and transmitting them as magically charged speech. During the 1950s and 1960s Spicer was an important presence in Los Angeles and San Francisco poetry networks. Like many writers of his generation, he noticed the relation of new technology to the imaginative process.

By the late 1940s radio had become a major medium nearly everywhere in America—the 45 rpm recording had recently been developed—and television was beginning to make its first invasions of our collective psyche. Spicer's antenna quickly picked up the connection between electromagnetic waves and the poet's mind.

Since 1950 electronic media have proliferated, the technical equipment has been streamlined and refined, radio and television are all-pervasive: it's difficult *not* to see or hear much so-called information continually arriving via unseen airwaves. Marshall McLuhan and others have covered the cosmic and historical aspects of these developments at length. What interests me as a postwar/TV baby and writer is how these changes have been assimilated into the work of my contemporaries.

I know plenty of very good poets who are just as familiar with the writings of Chuck Berry and Smokey Robinson as they are with those of Byron, Keats and Shelley. Bob Dylan's songs have come to be as much a part of our canon as Shakespeare's sonnets. There are interesting parallels among all these writers in their respective mastery of lyric forms. Such parallels between great literary poets and popular composers are common. My theory is that for numerous younger poets the radio rivals the book as a primary source of poetic information. As much conformity and mediocrity as there have always been in popular song, the classics of jazz and rhythm & blues (to name two rich indigenous modes of American music) have claimed the lasting power of masterpieces. A lot of poets born since the Second World War have been unconsciously absorbing such musical forms in ever greater volume over the intervening decades.

The sudden juxtapositions that can occur while turning the dial or changing TV channels have also instructed the bardic brain in new techniques of eclecticism. Sometimes the mind moves sideways in associative shifts that only the freedom of poetry can graph. Schizophrenese, the language spoken by people suffering certain psychic disturbances, is often rich with poetic insight but seldom displays the formal control embodied by the poet's craft. In its technical ability to receive such seemingly conflicting signals and give order to their diversity of voices, the radio's circuitry is analogous to the poet's multiple awareness.

Even on a less strictly technical, more literary level poetry and electronics have come some distance together. In 1949 a poet and pacifist named Lewis Hill created the first listener-sponsored noncommercial radio station anywhere. Hill and his colleagues called their venture Pacifica; the FM station's call letters were KPFA. Poetry, drama, public affairs, panel discussions of controversial topics, book reviews and other literate programming were integral from the beginning to KPFA's format. It was free-speech radio, supported entirely by listeners' subscriptions, and somehow it managed to survive the McCarthy and Cold War eras with its anarchist/pacifist principles intact.

While the San Francisco Renaissance and Beat movements were putting that city on the international literary map, KPFA in Berkeley was instrumental in airing the voices of most of the poets involved. Radio was an excellent medium for the new poetry because so much of the writing was "composed on the tongue," crafted with the spontaneity of oral expression. The Beat writers rescued American poetry from the formal confines of the printed page. They all first published their work at readings, and KPFA was often there to record and air this wild new poesy. Kenneth Rexroth was the station's resident literary critic and his intimate association with many of the arriving Bay Area writers was no doubt instrumental in creating the link between Pacifica, poetry and the public.

When Dylan Thomas made his legendary American tours in 1952 and '53, he appeared live on KPFA. It was largely his booming *basso profundo* which opened American minds to the fact that poetry is indeed a vocal form. As Robert Duncan, Allen Ginsberg, Lawrence Ferlinghetti and others gradually appeared on the scene, they reinforced and extended the idea of the poem as a spoken utterance. Although poetry still enjoys (and suffers) extensive life on the page, the work occurring in San Francisco in the mid-fifties—including the presence of KPFA as an instrument in disseminating that work—expanded the scope of what poets could do as cultural performers in this country.

And Pacifica broadened the range of radio. In addition to its own small network of stations (now in Berkeley, Los Angeles, Houston, Washington DC and New York City) KPFA eventually spawned the hundreds of public radio stations currently operating in communities throughout the United States. With the uniformity and narrowness of format found on most commercial stations, it has become the job of these alternative broadcasters to keep alive traditions that may be outside the commercial mainstream—musical traditions certainly, but also traditions of free speech and spoken arts.

"Poetry seems to have gotten us in trouble two or three times," says Pacifica historian Vera Hopkins. This is precisely why it is unfit for mainstream media. Poets with anything interesting to say inevitably offend some people. Sponsors (not to mention the FCC) don't like to upset the mythical "average" listener.

One of the more innovative programs I ever heard on KPFA was Pat Nolan and Andrei Codrescu's "Calling All Poets," which ran for much of 1975. "Calling All Poets" was a weekly phone-in open reading. Anyone whose receiver could pull in the station's 59,000-watt signal—meaning tens of thousands of listeners all over Northern California—was invited to call in and read a poem on the air. I wouldn't say it was a great show because the poetry for the most part was pretty shaky. Conceptually, however, it was brilliant in its attempt at literary-technological linkage. John Giorno in New York City had already established his Dial-a-Poem telephone service and was putting out anthology albums through Giorno Poetry Systems. Various little magazines had begun to come out as records and cassettes. Since then, CDs and videos and multimedia literary publications have proliferated. The bardic tradition has come full circle, returning to its oral origins by way of electronics. Through radio especially the human voice can reach where no book goes.

As we approach the year 2000 and the printed text faces serious challenges from other forms of information exchange, poets with any deep understanding of their art know that the ability to speak it is crucial to communication with a public beyond a small circle of initiates. Those of us who feel connected to current social and historical realities realize that if our mysterious news—news from the netherworld, the uncon-scious, "out there"—that if this numinous news is to be heard, we must know how to say our poetry aloud. Radio, or more accurately those radio frequencies which allow for the pres-ence of poets in public air, will be essential to keeping alive a tradition increasingly threatened on the page.

The common interweaving of the poet's spirit and the radio-muse intuited by Cocteau has evolved more rapidly and far-reachingly than even his lightning intelligence might have foreseen. Literally thousands of Orpheuses are now on the loose in the wired world, bridging the boundaries between public and intimate realms, between poetry and song, between this realm and the one beyond your radio.

1980

Antiwarism:
Should Poets Make a
Claim to Moral Clarity?

George W. Bush and his lovely wife, Laura, have done more to raise the profile of American poetry than any presidential couple since the Kennedys invited Robert Frost to read a poem at JFK's inauguration. Just as Frost was blinded by the glare off the January snow that icy afternoon in 1961, the first lady this past February was caught in a dazzling blizzard of "protest" poems after she'd invited a group of poets to the White House to celebrate the spirits of the safely dead Walt Whitman, Emily Dickinson and Langston Hughes. Getting wind of the live poets' intention of presenting her with their objections to her husband's impending war against Iraq, Mrs. Bush canceled the planned salon, proving, in the words of *The New York Times,* "that the most effective poetry reading is the one that never happens." The publicity generated by this nonevent made poets in this culture appear to be more potent than they really are.

If poetry, as W. H. Auden famously observed, "makes nothing happen," perhaps that was the point of the poets' gesture of opposition to the president's policies: to make the war not happen. As one of the more intimate and humanistic art forms, devoted to precise language, individual vision and truthful communication, poetry is naturally antipolitical and antiwar— politics and war being notorious breeding grounds for lies, clichés and euphemisms. So how radical or difficult is it, really, to write an "antiwar" poem? Virtually all poems, whatever their theme, are antiwar. The question is how clearly and truly they articulate experience or thought. The danger of assuming an artistic posture explicitly in opposition to the state is, in the very act of opposition, that of becoming a mirror image of official propaganda. Much of what passes for "protest" poetry is political rhetoric by another name—mobilized for a benign purpose perhaps but often shading into self-righteousness, proclaiming the virtue of the speaker as a champion of peace or justice and blaming the bad guys for everything that's wrong with the world—in this way resembling the good-versus-evil ideology of messianic moralizers like Bush and Osama bin Laden.

The most powerful and memorable antiwar poetry I know has been written not by protesters but witnesses. The English soldier-poet Wilfred Owen, fighting in the trenches of World War I; the Jewish German Paul Celan, who barely survived the Holocaust, and the Lithuanian Czeslaw Milosz, who worked with the Polish Resistance in World War II; the Palestinian Mahmoud Darwish, enduring the Israeli bombardment of Beirut in 1982—each of these, through charged, inventive language, unflinching perception and a ruthlessly self-questioning attitude, lays bare the pathos and contradiction and disorienting obscenity of organized violence. None speaks from a safe remove—Owen was killed on the battlefield at twenty-five— and none assumes a position of political omniscience or moral superiority. As human beings, they imply (as Camus does in *The Fall*), we are all guilty. It is this acknowledgment of the inner shadow, this grief in the face of moral disaster, combined with great linguistic originality, that gives these writers their richness of expression and depth of spiritual insight. The individuality and intimacy and inwardness of their vision, rather than condemnation of the *other*'s crimes, makes their art irrefutable in a way no strictly "political" utterance can touch.

But Mrs. Bush's dainty notion that literature should somehow be indifferent to or oblivious of history is absurd. Emily Dickinson may have been a visionary recluse, feeding on the genius of her own eccentric imagination, but to try to separate Whitman or Hughes from the turmoil of his times is ridiculous. Hughes deliberately set out to speak in a nonliterary idiom from the perspective and experience of "Negro" America, with all the pain and tragedy and defiant optimism of the black man's burden. And Whitman, for all his early expansive exuberance, was bitterly disillusioned by the moral horror of slavery, the nightmare of the Civil War (whose human casualties he witnessed firsthand as a nurse to the Union wounded), and the perversion of American freedom into a free-for-all of capitalistic greed. *Democratic Vistas*, his later prose testament, is still hopeful yet saturated with disappointment that "these States" were turning out to be grossly different from what he had originally envisioned. It is this mature recognition of America's failure to live up to its ideals that gives the younger Walt's enthusiasms their tragic poignancy. For the first lady, who as a librarian should know better, to airbrush away these critical aspects of our national poets is an act of willful ignorance worthy of the sneakiest Soviet censor.

The tendency to sentimentalize, to idealize, to simplify and purify an otherwise murky and ambiguous reality is typically the symptom of an ideological agenda, whatever wing of the political spectrum it may be serving. The mythification of "heroes," whether warriors or war resisters, is often an act of selective memory and must be subject to skeptical scrutiny lest we lose sight of the complexity of human character. People with firsthand experience of catastrophe are less inclined to sentimentality than those whose knowledge has been gained at a comfortable distance. A good example of this phenomenon is Roman Polanski's recent film *The Pianist*, a Holocaust survival drama whose protagonist endures a horrific ordeal mainly through dumb luck and the incidental decency of strangers (including one Nazi officer). Unlike Steven Spielberg's *Schindler's List,* which manipulates its viewers' emotions by cleaning up the character of Oskar Schindler into that of an admirable angel of mercy, Polanski's treatment of similar material is devoid of uplift—partly, no doubt, because the director himself as a child barely escaped with his life from Europe's collapse into fascism. Even the victims in *The Pianist* are depicted as flawed or grotesque, thus depriving the audience of the comfort of easy identification. History, he seems to be suggesting, has no good guys.

A great range of responses may complement each other in the mobilization of an antiwar esthetic. Preconceived notions of "moral clarity" (one of the president's favorite concepts) and/or sanctimonious militancy are imagination's enemies. Even apparently "escapist" art may serve a subversive or corrective purpose. Some twenty years ago in Santa Cruz, at the height of Ronald Reagan's nuke-rattling presidency and attendant fears for an imperiled world, the poet Gary Young was reading to a sizable audience one night; he read a delicate poem about his garden, and a heckler in the back of the hall called out, "How can you be reading poems about flowers when we're on the brink of a nuclear holocaust?" After a brief pause, Young replied, "I can't think of a better time." Which is to say that seemingly apolitical art can also evoke the values and pleasures that make the world worth saving and life worth savoring. Often such evocations of beauty can be an antidote to despair, just as anger and outrage can motivate and inform imaginative acts of resistance.

A week or so before Mrs. Bush disinvited the peace-mongering bards to her politically polite poetic tea, Secretary of State Colin Powell made his pitch for war against Iraq at the United Nations Security Council. As if to prove that art is more eloquent than even the most respected statesman's powers of persuasion, a reproduction of Picasso's *Guernica*—the painter's anguished denunciation of the Nazi bombing of civilians in the Spanish Civil War—was discreetly covered during Powell's speech. Such censorship only accentuates the threat that all art poses to official rhetoric. Like the child whose innocence exposes the emperor's nakedness, the artist is charged with unmasking collective illusions. Bombs and bombast may be more devastating than anyone's pen or brush, but the affirmation of creative witness, however powerless to save us from ourselves, may at least offer some pungent consolation.

For writers, finally, the only war worth fighting is the war against cliché.

2003

Seducing the Muse: Notes on the Nature of Inspiration

When Homer says, in the opening line of *The Odyssey*, "Tell me, Muse…" or, in another translation, "Sing in me, Muse, and through me tell the story…," he's asking to serve as a medium for a force greater than his personal powers of singing or story-telling. He's asking for inspiration, and he's offering himself as the instrument that will lift the breath of the poem into the air where it must finally take flight on its own. The poet, like the musician, applies his or her technical skills to the mysterious task of making something out of nothing—the word for poet in Greek is the same as the word for maker—and for this he needs the help of a faithful muse.

Muse—music. Inspiration—breath. Poet—maker. These are three corners of the creative triangle out of which poetry rises. If the gods of the classical era are not quite so available to our twenty-first-century spirits, poets still know that they need their muses, and each one must cultivate an intimate way of invoking that vital presence. When your muse is with you, your language moves with ease—though not without effort—from one word, one line, to the next. The combinations of sounds and syllables, rhythms and images begin to fall into patterns that have a life of their own beyond your writing them down, and yet they require your active role as an accomplice. The poem unfolds.

Sometimes it's that straightforward and spontaneous—"First thought, best thought," as Allen Ginsberg put it. At other times it's as William Butler Yeats described in "Adam's Curse": "…A line will take us hours maybe; / Yet if it does not seem a moment's thought, / Our stitching and unstitching has been naught." Whether it comes in a flash of grace or only through draft after draft of meticulous revision, the goal is to make the poem seem inevitable, as if it couldn't be any other way. The crafty maker creates the illusion of utter naturalness, so that even the rhymes, those patterns of echoing sounds and reflective images, go almost unnoticed in the larger movement of the composition. The poem takes wing on its own combination of strength and lightness. And the muse, that sneaky co-conspirator, is nowhere in sight.

So the muse is something like a natural resource to which the poet goes in order to draw what he or she needs to convert to song. In more mundane or psychological terms, the muse is an ideal reader beyond and within the writer, a sympathetic reader who both understands and casts an illusionless eye on the writer's text. Is it honestly imagined? Does it tell the truth in the sense of going deeper than mere fact into some universal zone of experience? Does it resonate with reality, however much it may sacrifice conventional ways of seeing and expression? Does it have a voice that's unique yet within the tradition, absorbing and transforming what's been done before? Does it bring across a body of ideas or themes or feelings that can't be paraphrased? The muse is merciless in demanding the most conscientious application of the poet's powers to harvest from their collaboration a singular and revelatory document, a testimony to their intimacy.

The poem itself is the only accurate description of how this happens. It records the process as it forms the result. If the muse is pleased, a certain radiance beams from the page; a certain resonance surrounds the saying of the lines. We say the work is inspired, that it moves us, that it shows us something we didn't know before and may not be able to explain, but we feel its glow inside us. We're changed. Our molecules are rearranged. We look at the world—and at words—in a different way. We feel refreshed.

Unless we were very lucky, it wasn't like this in high-school English. There, if we heard a poem spoken aloud, it was only to analyze its hidden meanings—as if it didn't mean what it said and how it sounded on the surface. True, the nature of metaphor is to compare one thing to another—that's how poems mean *more* than what they say—but sometimes a cigar is just a cigar, stinky or aromatic, cancerous or transcendental, streaming its ribbon of smoke uniquely in a form that can't be captured even on film. The marvel of a great poem, like that of a great piece of music, is that its greatness can never be explained as well or as eloquently as it explains itself. Just listen.

That's what the poet does: He or she listens and looks, and smells and tastes and feels and reflects, and waits for the words to arrive. It's an active waiting, an active listening, a poised receptiveness that registers changes of light, of tone, of anything the senses perceive or the mind imagines. In the shifting rhythms of experience, in the wondrous and frightening revelations of dreams, in the details of everyday life, the muse is looming, subtly asking to be seduced, and the poet's obligation is to respond. It may mean taking a journey whose dangers you'd just as soon not face; you may encounter sides of yourself you'd prefer not to know. But the joy of exploring, whatever its risks, is in discovering where you need to go.

There's a musical composition by Thelonious Monk called "Ugly Beauty." That kind of paradoxical beauty can also be true of a poem: it may show us something we'd rather not have seen, and yet, in its disclosure, it has a way of being transformed into something perhaps more beautiful than its subject matter or original impression suggested. Its dissonance—as in Monk's distinctive music—shakes us out of our laziness, makes us look and listen for what we never meant to notice but which enlarges and enriches the world we know, and we're grateful to have been driven beyond our limits. We find, in fact, that our limits are fictitious, just as the possible ways to write a poem are nearly limitless.

Consider that the soaring rhetoric of such virtuosos as Wallace Stevens and Dylan Thomas exists on equal terms in the same world with the more colloquial, conversational, down-to-earth voices of William Carlos Williams and Charles Bukowski. That the longwinded exhibitionism of a Walt Whitman can exist in the same poetic universe with the lyrical modesty of an Emily Dickinson, or the hard-edged Modernism of an Ezra Pound with the extravagant Romanticism of an Edna St. Vincent Millay, feels almost to be a miracle. All of these masters and many more are writers whose visions and poetics seem at first glance to be mutually exclusive, yet any poet can learn a lot from each of them. It is only through reading the widest possible range of poetries, and reading them as deeply as we can, that we finally synthesize a working, breathing poetics of our own.

Poetry is the most democratic of arts: anyone can write, or try to write; all it takes is a sheet of paper and a pen or pencil. Or maybe not even that; leaving aside the computer screen and other paperless gadgets, consider the method of William Wordsworth, taking long walks and composing poems in his head. Whatever one's personal process, the mind must be still enough to receive the words, and must master the skills to select them carefully and set them down in order. It takes a good deal of discipline. It takes a certain humility. It takes a certain courage or daring. Like cooking or kissing, it takes practice. But it tastes so good.

2003

A Note on the Author

Stephen Kessler is a poet, translator, essayist and editor whose writings have appeared in books, anthologies, magazines and newspapers across the United States since the late 1960s. Born in Los Angeles in 1947, he has degrees in literature from Bard College and the University of California, Santa Cruz. He is the author of eight books and chapbooks of original poetry and more than a dozen books of poetry and fiction in translation, including *Written in Water: The Prose Poems of Luis Cernuda,* which received a 2004 Lambda Literary Award. He was a founding editor and publisher of *Alcatraz,* an international journal, and *The Sun,* a Santa Cruz weekly, among other periodicals and independent publishing ventures. He is a contributing editor of *Poetry Flash* and the editor of *The Redwood Coast Review.* For more about Stephen Kessler visit www.stephenkessler.com.